Truth Across the Waters

Admiral Bill Schachte
The Admiral Who Changed America

W. THOMAS MCQUEENEY

Palmetto Publishing GroupCharleston, SC

Truth Across the Waters

Copyright © 2020 by W. Thomas McQueeney

All rights reserved

No portion of this book may be reproduced, stored in a retrieval system, or transmitted in any form by any means–electronic, mechanical, photocopy, recording, or other–except for brief quotations in printed reviews, without prior permission of the author.

First Edition

Printed in the United States

ISBN-13: 978-1-64111-716-6
ISBN-10: 1-64111-716-8

Cover Page: Lieutenant junior grade William Leon Schachte, Jr., surveying the shoreline at Cam Rahn Bay, Vietnam in 1968. Courtesy of Schachte Family Archives.

TRUTH ACROSS THE WATERS
The Admiral Who Changed America

*Portrait of Rear Admiral Upper Half William Leon Schachte, Jr.
Oil on canvas by Rubenstein Brown.*

W. Thomas McQueeney, Author

Acknowledgements

Biographies are both difficult and simple. One might assume that the simple would win out because the overabundance of information in modern times is readily available. Yet there is the arduous task of reassembling and compiling timelines and, importantly, the insights of the main character—the person of historical note who lived those facts.

In the case of Rear Admiral William Leon Schachte, Jr., there were advantages. The admiral lived not too far from the author. He was accessible. He was congenial, and he was most helpful in providing personal artifacts, saved articles, and old photos. But even in these exercises, there has to be another element that builds the objectivity of the shadow character of the effort—truth. To find truth, there had to be established trust on a two-way street. Having known the Schachte family for more than fifty years, trust emerged quickly as a foundation of an enjoyable process.

The admiral has associations with key contributors across the country. It is with sincere appreciation that communications were established with the admiral's former Navy Vietnam successor and accomplished author John O'Neill. O'Neill, a scholar, lawyer, and Naval Academy graduate, was an invaluable source of Vietnam era information. His bestseller, *Unfit for Command*, is a landmark publication related to politics and the Vietnam era.

The admiral introduced me to another friend, retired Navy JAG Captain Joe Baggett. In multiple exchanges, Baggett was able to clarify and even edit several passages. It is a credit to him that he took much of his personal time and interest to assist the effort. His talent and direction proved invaluable.

My friendship with the internationally-recognized artist Mary Whyte has been propitious. She has authored several books and has taught me much about visuals and presentation. Mary Whyte proved to be much more than the world's pre-eminent watercolor artist. If it is even possible, her perch was heightened in my eyes, in every regard.

Retired Marine Corps Lieutenant Colonel Frederick Whittle became a personal friend decades ago. Whittle's historical perspective, editing skills, and general insight to the entire project in this volume are inestimable. This book would not be possible without Fred Whittle's selfless and timely contributions. He is a highly-respected friend.

Someday, historians will look back at the life of Admiral Bill Schachte and find profound inspiration in his contributions to the United States Navy, to international maritime law, to the legal profession, to military justice, to U.S. intelligence, and to setting the record straight concerning false claims of a presidential candidate. His willingness to stand up for truth changed America.

Dedication

This work is dedicated to my wife Carmen. Our Lord works in mysterious ways. When Carmen and I celebrated our 50th anniversary we enjoyed guests—a husband and wife duet—who were fabulous singers. They picked the songs. One song that they sang was from the musical South Pacific. That song, Some Enchanted Evening can easily describe the way that I met Carmen at the Naval Officers Club at Roosevelt Roads, Puerto Rico. That meeting was profoundly enchanted. Carmen has amazing intelligence, ready humor, constructive criticism when warranted, grace, and a positive attitude. In a sense, she has co-authored my adult life. As the words drifted out on that anniversary evening, "Once you have found her, never let her go," I realized that we were meant to be together always.

In remembrance, I want to add a tribute to my parents Bill and Mary Schachte. Their respect and love for each other spoke volumes to our close Charleston family.

Admiral William L. Schachte

TRUTH ACROSS THE WATERS

Introduction

Truth comes from above. A deep understanding of the value of and devotion to truth is an admirable human character trait, and an indispensable lodestar of inspired civil society. Like the rain from the heavens, truth trickles into the brooks and streams of human activity to larger repositories. The rivers take it to the seas and the oceans of our communal existence. It sustains the good life. Without truth, there is much more dysphoria.

A life built upon truth is often a life of challenge, when much is at stake. The life of Admiral William L. Schachte, Jr., navigates the waters of truth in a world where shoals of malfeasance are all too common. From Vietnam Swift Boats—to the Black Sea Incident with the Soviet Russians—to the infamous Tailhook Scandal—one man of character connects all three events. He fought in America's most controversial war, advised our national leaders on international maritime law, and insisted upon proper military decorum throughout his beloved U.S. Navy. Political historians will validate that Admiral Schachte likely changed the outcome of a U.S. presidential election. He did so by speaking truth to power. It was his duty, as he saw it, and not a choice. Our republic's very health depends upon a commitment to the truth.

The admiral understood the systems.

He maneuvered vessels, sequenced return fire upon enemy combatants, and—sadly—delivered condolences to families grieving from the loss of loved ones. He earnestly applied himself to his naval career. After receiving his law degree, he engaged in other studies—a master's program in international law. His work in the maritime legal framework, set forth in the United Nations *Convention on the Law of the Sea,* established his credentials in the resolution of flashpoint global matters. His prowess advanced his career into the Naval Investigative Service where his guidance reconciled several landmark determinations, including the cause of the explosion on the USS Iowa. The forty-first U.S. president, George H. W. Bush, affirmed Schachte's appointment as the Navy's acting Judge Advocate General and the administration of 1,100 JAG lawyers. The admiral arrived with a new docket—to adjudicate an excruciating episode of predatory crimes perpetrated in a Las Vegas hotel. The Tailhook Scandal would create horrific media controversy, entail just and hefty punishments, and change the culture of the United States Navy forever. In these occurrences and throughout his career, truth was his indispensable ally.

Schachte retired after more than thirty years in the service of the country. His work in private law practice ensued with the vigor of his former duty. It was a new life of resolve in the pursuit of truth.

Truth applied in the public sector presented myriad new challenges for the admiral. These could involve media confrontation, controversy in the political arena, and the magnification of public scrutiny. Admiral Schachte never wavered from his established baseline. Truth trumps all else.

The north star of our journey through life has no earthly arrival. The grace-filled balance sheet of our actions, inactions, and intentions tally to a higher authority—and a higher rank than a two-star rear admiral. To that end, Bill Schachte stayed at the helm faithfully and guided an unwavering course.

Table of Contents

Acknowledgements · v
Dedication · vii
Introduction · ix
Prologue · xv

Chapter 1	Between the Ashley and the Cooper · · · · · · · · · · · · · · ·	1
Chapter 2	Upon Charleston Harbor · · · · · · ·	23
Chapter 3	The Clemson Years · · · · · · · · · · ·	30
Chapter 4	The Navy Option · · · · · · · · · · · · ·	37
Chapter 5	Carmen for a Lifetime · · · · · · · · · ·	46
Chapter 6	Swift Boats on the South China Sea · · · · · · ·	60
Chapter 7	In the Crosshairs · · · · · · · · · · · · · · · · ·	74
Chapter 8	The Return of the Sailor · · · · · · · · · · · · ·	78
Chapter 9	Directed Sadness, Rochester · · · · · · · · · · ·	82
Chapter 10	A Tiger in Gamecock Land · · · · · · · · · · · ·	90
Chapter 11	International Law Expertise · · · · · · · · · · ·	94
Chapter 12	The Pulse of the Pentagon · · · · · · · · · · ·	102
Chapter 13	After Impact: The Black Sea Resolution · · · · · · ·	123
Chapter 14	NIS—Naval Investigative Service · · · · · · · · · · ·	127
Chapter 15	The 60 Minutes Interview · · · · · · · · · · · · ·	132
Chapter 16	Tailhooks of Intolerance · · · · · · · · · · · · · ·	145
Chapter 17	Private Life in the Holy City · · · · · · · · · · · ·	154
Chapter 18	Coming Around Again · · · · · · · · · · · · · · · ·	163
Chapter 19	Reprint: The Interview that Changed an Election · · · · · ·	180

Chapter 20	What Next?	196
Chapter 21	In God's Hands	206

Postscript · 216
About the Author · 221
Endnotes · 222

Truth Across the Waters

Admiral Bill Schachte
An American Biography

Before the Fifth: Parents Bill and Mary Schachte holding baby Frank.
Sitting L to R: Kay, Margie and Bill.
Photo from 1948.
Younger brother Joe was born in 1952.

Prologue

Admirals eventually leave the bridge, the desk, and the podium. They retire. Occasionally, they show up for commemorations, anniversaries, and funerals. Their lives place them upon the waters—their bays are of enemy fire, their seas of distress, and their gulfs present challenges to our free country. They are disciplined for battle. They emerge. They direct. They succeed. And sometimes they reflect. This volume is a chronological reflection of an admiral who mattered in the synchronicity of his country.

In their trade, admirals survey more of the earth in their navigations—an aqueous surface nearly two and a half times more than the land area of our globe. Yet, it is the land we laymen know best. It is the land surface that we acclimate, accommodate, and accentuate.

William Leon Schachte, Jr., was born on May 1, 1940. It was propitious that he was raised by a supportive family of achievers—in a place where achievement was most difficult.

Charleston, South Carolina, of the 1940s was still on the hundred-year backslide of a war the old southern city initiated. April 12, 1861 was seventy-eight years past the Treaty of Paris ending the American Revolution, but only four-score years prior to the throes of World War II. The advent of the second great war would not seem to be a suitable time for Mary and Bill Schachte, Sr. to welcome their second child. Wars are, by definition, unsettling.

Charleston had spent the better part of a century trying to overcome an image problem. What Charlestonians term the "War of Northern

Aggression" began early at a pre-dawn hour with the firing upon Fort Sumter. Those Yanks just wouldn't leave peacefully! In due course, the Union soldiers returned with punitive intent. The siege of Charleston lasted 567 days—still the longest siege of a city in world history.[1] The rubble became a lot of trouble.

Charleston was once the belle of the ball. The first major southern port utilized by those high-masted ships of yesteryear was Charleston—the fourth-largest city in America by the calculations of our nation's first census in 1790.[2]

At the time of that initial 4:30 a.m. volley of 1861, Charleston was still the sixth-largest city in the United States.[3] By the 1940[4] census, Charleston was not listed in the top 100 populated cities. The fall was painful.

Reconstruction even missed the Holy City. There was not enough money to do anything other than to repair and paint from the ruins with cheap or homemade products. Pieces of some buildings were used to piece together other buildings.

The economic drivers of rice and cotton had diminished because the former slave labor force had been propitiously emancipated. Plantations became tenant farms, unsuited for wealth creation. Merchants, contractors, and other professionals eked out an existence under dire economic conditions. Many Charlestonians moved away from depressed surroundings. Little would improve in their lifetimes. It was much like trying to grow a healthy crop on fields blighted by a storm-forced saltwater tide. Futility undermined most efforts.

Hope existed in the hearts of those who stayed. Charlestonians were mannerly people who had lost everything but their dignity. They huddled against hard times. Their protection was their decency and their descendance from past glories. They had the pride of yesterday in reserve—awaiting the promise of tomorrow.

Some timely events gave a hint of that promise.

It was the Department of the Navy that brought a modicum of upsurge by the need for ship repairs and strategic base stationing in 1904.[5] Charleston was critical to American protection in the South Atlantic and Caribbean corridor. The deep-water harbor sustained the city's desolate workforce by the incidence of another war (Spanish-American) — and then another (the then-monikered "Great War"). The Charleston Navy Yard became a busy economic driver. World War II was over two decades away.

Among the top engineers at the naval facility was a young family man, William Leon Schachte. The bright shipyard engineer and his wife Mary were beginning a family in 1939. The ship repair business was steady. The warship business was about to begin.

The senior Schachte made that thriving corner of the Holy City's desolate economy into a career that vaulted him, eventually, to the highest local level. The Schachte name would become prominent in the civilian circles of the Navy's presence.

When his oldest son, young Billy Schachte was only a year-and-a-half of age, the United States became embroiled in a war of three oceans and six continents. Charleston was immediately strategically important again. The rule of the seas depended, in part, upon the tireless efforts of those patriotic Confederate progeny. Charlestonians had long been resourceful and self-reliant. They were all too willing to recompose their patriotism in chivalric concordance with a nation in need.

The waters are the highway of the world. Again, Charleston would enter the international stage from its deep, natural harbor. The Schachte family would rise in consequence.

The expectation of self-reliance and personal responsibility became central to the Schachte family's character. Character was everything. A person's integrity would be considered vastly superior to other assets such as a stately home, a healthy bank account, or a finishing school education. The Schachtes embodied this sacred law of living rightly. There was no prevarication, no equivocation, and no misrepresentation. Above all else, what was demanded in the Schachte household was truthful living.

Truth would provide the critical summation of the journey across the waters.

CHAPTER 1
Between the Ashley and the Cooper

A local adage in Charleston has been that the Ashley and Cooper Rivers converge to form the Atlantic Ocean. It's an egocentric thought that even makes Charlestonians blush a bit. The 1670 arrival of *The Adventure* from England brought an excellent complement of builders, farmers, and militia. The next three and half centuries, to the present time, would produce a new country, a failed Confederacy, and a renaissance of grandiose proportions.

Those sine-wave decades of moderate prosperity and paucity produced Charleston families of notable achievement. The Schachte family met challenges as leadership needs arose.

Billy Schachte's parents weathered the Great Depression, an economic calamity that was more severe in Charleston than in most places. A city without growth, meaningful industry, and the swelter of summers without air conditioning was especially difficult. Port trade was inconsistent. The infrastructure was nearly Third World with inadequate sewers, un-administered dumping grounds, and a patchy road system accentuated by spartan bridges. They were built for transit but were too often utilized by those departing the city forever. Tourism was scant. Only the diehards lived in the Holy City. As difficult as it was, the old mansions survived, the old families persevered, and the old hopes remained. The Schachtes were stalwarts.

Schachte's mother, Mary (nee) Farmer, met his father when he was at Clemson College. Clemson was then a military, engineering, and agricultural school tucked away into the trace foothills of the Blue Ridge Mountains.

The young Miss Farmer was awarded a scholarship to Anderson College where she became the freshman class president. It was not the norm for southern women to have college opportunities in the early to mid-1900s. But Anderson College had a fine pedigree. It had roots as Johnson Female Seminary (Baptist) in 1848.[6] That facility closed during the Civil War and reopened in 1870 as a female-only college, Johnson University, eventually renamed as Anderson College. The college remained all-female until 1931.[7]

Mary Farmer's academic pursuit was similar to many women of that era. They were trained to teach. Her discipline was early childhood education.

The loss of revenues of many American colleges related to the Great War (World War I) opened placements for women in other colleges.

In upstate South Carolina, a grant from a wealthy Massachusetts businessman, Robert C. Winthrop, started Winthrop College, ostensibly for the need of teachers in the south.[8] Both of Mary Farmer's older sisters graduated from Winthrop. By contrast, the College of Charleston (founded 1770[9]) was populated by an all-male student body until 1918. The Great War eventually led to a need for female students there to continue the college's academic mission and buoy its lagging finances. Despite these exceptions, women had limited opportunities in the American South in the first half of the twentieth century.

Billy Schachte recalled the family history.

"Mother's sisters both graduated from Winthrop College. The first to do so was Annice, her oldest sister—and when she finished, Annice helped my mother's second-oldest sister, Marjorie. We called her 'Aunt Jree.' Instead of following to Winthrop, Mother received a scholarship to Anderson College—where she graduated. These ladies who went to colleges in those days were truly rarities. It was something special that they were doing at that time—a family focus upon education in the early to late 1920s. Formal education was critical to their upbringing."

Mary Farmer was an excellent student and became a credit to the burgeoning reputation of Anderson College—a cozy campus less than twenty miles from Clemson. Clemson was within walking distance. Her future husband confirmed that dynamic.

Clemson had a thriving military corps of cadets, mostly manned by students from South Carolina. It appealed to families in Charleston because the college had diverse courses of study and was cooled naturally by the elevation away from the Atlantic Ocean. Admiral Schachte's grandfather graduated as an Electrical Engineering major at Clemson in 1907. His father, Bill Sr., enrolled at Clemson in 1930. The senior Schachte graduated from the former Clemson corps of cadets in 1934. He was an Electrical Engineering major, as well. The legacy was strong.

The admiral's father had a keen eye for bright and eloquent women in those early Depression years. Mary Farmer caught his full attention.

Commissioning of naval ship in Charleston Harbor by Mary Farmer Schachte. Attendees include Schachte's sister, Margie (L). Photo courtesy of Schachte family archives.

Schachte recalled the household story. "My dad used to lead the Clemson dance band known as the 'Jungleers.' He often told me one of the hardest things he had to do was to stand up there leading the band as he looked out on the dance floor and saw my mother dancing with other cadets. He was on-duty with the band.

"He also told me that he and a fellow cadet friend had gone to Anderson where my mother lived at the time. The friend apparently had too much to drink and forgot to come by and pick up my Dad to take him back to Clemson. Daddy finally realized he had been left and knew the only way to get back to Clemson was to walk—which he did. He proceeded on a 17-mile night-time walk mostly uphill. He said it was amazing 'watching the sun come up over the campus as he neared Clemson.'" Schachte related.

A romance had developed in the foothills to the Blue Ridge Mountains. The senior Schachte remained single-minded. He would sacrifice his sleep and his shoe leather to see young Mary Farmer again.

"There were two realizations I preened from his story. First, he had fallen in love with my mother. And he knew to be responsible—even in the face of adversity. Daddy set many character-building examples for our family," Schachte reminisced.

After finishing Clemson in 1934, the brilliant young engineer would ask for Mary's hand in marriage. As both were educated and enterprising, they would embark upon their life in a place far away from the Holy City—Pittsfield, Massachusetts. The Pittsfield GE Plant opened in 1903.[10] Both would soon come back to the Lowcountry of South Carolina.

"My sister, Kay—the oldest in my family—was born in Lynn, Massachusetts, while Daddy was working at the General Electric plant. They then came back to Charleston where Daddy got a job at the Naval Shipyard working as an electrician's helper in 1939. The rest of the children—starting with me—were all born in Charleston."

When Bill and Mary Schachte grew their family on the upper peninsula, they attended Sacred Heart Parish. The red-brick Charleston Catholic church was built in 1920.[11] to service the newer neighborhoods of that era.

The elder Schachtes imparted much wisdom to their five children in the lessons of faith, determination, and character. Those children had the benefit of an Eagle Scout father and an educationally-oriented mother.

"Mother was more the disciplinarian, and Daddy the industrious parliamentarian," Schachte asserted. "They were a great team."

He set the childhood experience details upon time and place.

"The oldest child was my sister, Kay, who became a nurse. Then there was me, then Margie—who became a *Miss Charleston*—then Frank and Joe. Three boys and two girls—all growing up at 152 Grove Street in a home with one bathroom.

"My Dad decked the second floor; it became somewhat like a dormitory. He also put a pool table up there. My father could do anything. He did all that by himself and took pride in the process of providing it. Once, he made an electric lawn mower using a motor from a discarded washing machine," Schachte recalled. "He had that kind of an engineering mindset. And he was confident to confront a challenge head-on."

The Schachte family emerged upon a path to success. They inherently pursued the best of the American dream.

"My Dad had one brother and one sister. His younger brother, Henry, was a real hero in our family. When Henry Schachte retired, he was the number one person at the international marketing firm, J. Walter Thompson. He had a home on the French Riviera, a place in Connecticut, and another on Fifth Avenue in New York. He was a real inspiration to all of us—and he had a wonderful sense of humor. He was a quiet, pleasant man—and extremely successful—and yet, a humble person."

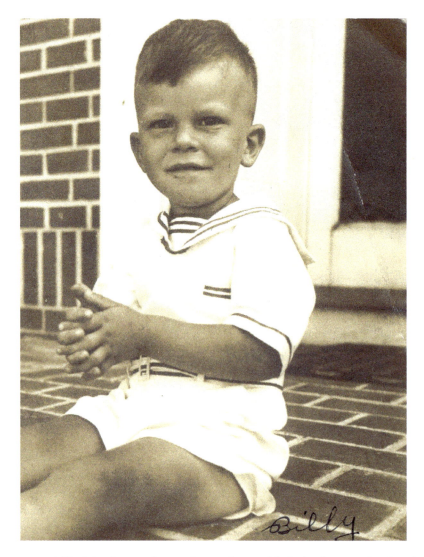

Young Billy Schachte ready to take on the world. (Schachte Family Photo)

There was a history that laced in Massachusetts to South Carolina. Schachte's grandfather was not the first of the family from Charleston to work in the Bay State. He left Clemson in 1907 for Pittsfield, Massachusetts. But Charleston was home.

Charleston roots are slow to grow but hard to kill. What the admiral recalled of that emigration and transition back to the Lowcountry revealed other family associations.

"Unfortunately, my grandfather was afflicted with Parkinson's Disease in the days before there was health insurance. At one point in his life, it was recommended that he move back south to see if the warmer temperatures and scent from pine trees would help his health. He and my grandmother moved to Summerville, South Carolina."

Summerville's restorative history was related to the belief that the pine trees were conducive to better health. In 1888, the International Congress of Physicians named Summerville as one of the two healthiest places on earth.[12]

"Growing up, my Dad was an Eagle Scout in Pittsfield. When it came time for him to go to college he was influenced by his father's educational experience. He subsequently applied to Clemson. In order to get there in those days he built his own car. He had an old frame for a Model-T Ford. He did some work on it, fixed it up and drove it from Pittsfield, Massachusetts to Clemson, South Carolina. I think it took at least four or five days back then. When Daddy graduated in 1934, he followed in his father's footsteps back to Pittsfield," Schachte explained.

There was family in Pittsfield and others in South Carolina. The trip from Pittsfield to Charleston is nearly 1000 miles.

"My grandfather had three brothers," Schachte explained. "That family arrived in Charleston in the 1800's. Frank and Emile Comer, my grandfather's first cousins, went to Pittsfield from Charleston and met my grandmother who had some sisters. Frank married one of the sisters, Ruth, and Emile Comer married another sister, Florence. They all came back to Charleston. Charleston had that welcoming attraction even back then."

Eventually, and with the advent of air conditioning, Charleston dominated as a destination. The young Schachte family was permanently at home on Grove Street.

*St. Francis Xavier Hospital, built in 1926.
The Schachtes supported the maternity ward often enough.
Courtesy of archival photos from the Sisters of Charity of Our Lady of Mercy.*

"My mother, Mary Farmer Schachte, was an incredible lady and a compelling influence on my life and that of my brother and sisters. She met my Dad on a blind date at the time he was a cadet at Clemson. I believe he was in his junior year. Mother came from a family of four, two older sisters and she had a twin—a brother—my Uncle Joe. He died in his forties of lung cancer. It struck us that Mother's name was Mary and her twin brother was Joseph. It was truly Biblical."

Mary Schachte set standards.

"I never heard my mother say anything bad about anyone. She always taught us not to say anything about somebody if you can't say something good about them—and she lived by that," Schachte recalled proudly.

He reflected upon the warmth of the setting he experienced growing up in Charleston.

"In our family of five children on Grove Street we had a wonderful home and family life. My mom and dad were at the center of that. Mother provided delicious meals. For example, every Saturday we would have for lunch, or actually what southerners called 'dinner' as our main meal on Saturday—spaghetti. 'Supper' was a smaller meal in the evening. Mother would prepare all of the ingredients for her homemade spaghetti, like chopping tomatoes, mixing in the condiments, the meatballs, and then she would cook it for quite a while on Saturday morning. We would usually eat around one or two o'clock. I guess we had the same schedule that others had.

"In the evenings we had to be back in the house when the street lights came on. I was once late in coming back after the lights came on. I think I was at Hampton Park and was just delayed playing with friends. By the time I got home, my oldest sister, Kay, had been given my pork chop. If you weren't there on time, it was at your peril. It was a lesson learned," Schachte recalled.

"We always had roast beef dinner on Sunday after Mass at our parish church, Sacred Heart. It was sometimes with several guests, mostly Citadel cadets when my sisters got a little older. Some of them came to the Catholic Mass. I was an altar boy for ten years and was kneeling at the altar every Sunday."

Discipline was a constant for the Schachtes.

My sweet mother could be a pretty stern disciplinarian when she needed to be. My father had a Boy Scout belt that he had made. It was a broad leather belt that Mother kept in his closet at the ready. She didn't hesitate to use it if one of us deserved it—and that was me, often enough. The things I got in trouble for doing saved the others the punishment because they saw the result.

*Son Billy with his mother Mary Farmer Schachte in 1958.
Photo courtesy of Schachte family.*

"My mother was a Catholic convert. She had been a Methodist. She told me that once she asked Daddy about the Catholic church and faith after they had retired for the evening. He talked to her until about 6:00 a.m. about his faith and the Catholic church—and especially his love for the Catholic faith. She later told me that if she knew he would talk so much, she would have asked him about it on some Saturday mid-morning, so he wouldn't keep her awake all night." Schachte related.

His father had a strong and unwavering faith. It served the family well.

"When my father died unexpectedly and suddenly at age 59 from a heart attack, I had been back from Vietnam about a year. I got emergency leave to come to Charleston to be with my mother, and my brothers and sisters. We arrived with my dear wife, Carmen, and our young son, Billy," Schachte recalled the sad time.

"I was so impressed with my mother at that awful time. She remained strong throughout the services and visits from others. She was a rock. My father's wake was one of the biggest they ever had at the Catholic funeral home at the time on Wentworth Street. He had a top position in his career and countless life-long friends. We were all distraught when we got there. The first thing my mother did was hug me. She said, 'Billy, that's not him, he's not there, he is in heaven' as we looked at my Dad in the casket. Then as people would come by and hug her and express condolences, many friends and relatives were emotional. That made it a little more difficult for me to be the strong oldest son. Mother remained as my father would have expected—very comforting to all, kind and sweet, but extraordinarily sorrowful. But few would've known her profound sorrow. She would not let it show." Schachte retold.

His mother was able to brave the difficulties and assume the matriarchal mantel that would define the rest of her life.

A formal photo from high school. (Schachte family archives.)

"Mother and Daddy set a tone for my marriage. They loved each other for a lifetime. They were devoted to each other. And they focused that love to their five children. I'm fortunate that I was able to find that special person just as my father did," Schachte observed.

"Undoubtedly, the other most influential person in my life has been my dear wife, Carmen. She was always with me on every major decision we made, and we made most of those together concerning our future and our life. And when I volunteered for Vietnam, Carmen didn't fully understand, but supported my decision," Schachte rekindled the memory.

His parents exemplified other qualities. The Charleston mentality of getting by on what was needed as opposed to anything lavish or opulent ruled their new life together. It was how his parents had been able to flourish. The early years with their parents left quite a legacy for all five siblings.

Schachte shared other blessings.

"My dad was undoubtedly the most influential adult in my life. His Clemson experience gave us the impetus to seek the highest level of education we could obtain. His 1934 graduation was somewhat rare—and grandfather's 1907 degree was even rarer. And imagine that they were both electrical engineering majors," Schachte reminded. "That had to be a difficult course of study."

The emphasis of education worked out well for the bright father-engineer.

"As it turned out, my father ended up as the senior civilian employee in the naval shipyard. At the time, I think there were over 6,500 employees. His title was Chief Design Engineer. He also got his engineering branch involved in nuclear work with nuclear submarines and some other engineering feats. He was truly a leader." Schachte stated proudly.

"And while my dad was growing up with my disabled grandfather, his family was very dependent on the other Schachte brothers and their father, my great-grandfather. That was the first Henry Schachte. His name is still prominent in Charleston," Schachte noted.

"Schachte" became a generational name of importance in Charleston. Photo emblem courtesy of Charleston Historical Society.

"Henry Schachte and Sons Real Estate and Insurance was founded by my great-grandfather in 1881. They were a successful firm. I imagine they paid a lot of claims in 1886—the year of the great Charleston earthquake. My growing up years gave my siblings and me some degree of notoriety being a direct descendent," Schachte explained. "The name of the company stayed many years past its founder, my great-grandfather, who was also known as a devout Catholic."

The 1881 company still exists in Charleston, though through two merger iterations.

The first Henry Schachte was born in 1850 and died in 1930.[13] His son, William Leon Schachte, the admiral's grandfather, married Susie Adeline Miner in Boston on August 12, 1910.[14] It was his medical condition that fostered a move back to the Lowcountry—where the Schachte name was already well-known.

The Charleston legacy of Schachtes began with Henry Schachte (1850-1930). Henry Schachte and Sons Real Estate and Insurance became part of the Charleston streetscape. Photo courtesy Schachte family archives.

The admiral continued to detail the family history. The family bond extended to other communities.

"My Uncle Henry (the great-nephew and namesake of the first Henry Schachte) used to tell the story of going to the local grocery store in Pittsfield to get groceries. They would run a tab and eventually, the grocer would indicate that he had to pay the balance. My grandmother would contact Charleston, and they would send her a check. They had a very, very difficult time. But my dad never talked about that. He would talk about how he lost his father at an early age. My grandfather died in the early 1930s," Schachte recounted. "His father, my great-grandfather Henry Schachte died at nearly the same time, in 1930."

The admiral never knew his fraternal grandfather. But he knew the stories. His father became the focal point of most family conversations. The respect and admiration remain evident.

"My dad was also head of the Professional Engineers Society locally. He was, without a doubt, the smartest person I ever knew. I recall during World War II that Daddy had spent a lot of time at Dupont Station outside of Charleston. He was working with some other engineers on this new concept they called 'radar.' The advancements they were making in collaboration with the British became instrumental in saving London during the German Blitzkrieg. The radar stations provided early warning all around the British Isles. Consequently, my dad was exempt from military service because of his intricate work on national security projects," Schachte explained. "It was a good thing. He did so much to save so many lives."

By his collaborative work, he indirectly impacted many lives in the Battle of Britain. It was the detection of the German Luftwaffe by radar that alerted the British Royal Air Force into defensive action.

The admiral's engineer-father remained attentive to his primary responsibilities as a father and husband. By his effort, the Grove Street home life had a rich basis of spirituality.

"Daddy and Mother were very devout Catholics in a very understanding way. They led by example the way they lived their lives. I never heard either one of them say anything unkind about anyone.

The household had stringent rules. The Schachte family would embrace discipline from these early foundation days of 1950's Charleston.

"Growing up, my sister Kay and I were the oldest, and we got the biggest load of the discipline. We had to be in on the weekends no later than 10 p.m. That rule was even after Kay graduated from high school. She was in nursing school, but the rule prevailed because she was staying at home. Kay and I remind Margie, Frank, and Joe that they had it a lot easier." Schachte indicated a smile.

"Like many of the Charleston teenagers around me, I had a paper route. It was an afternoon route. It was in a minority neighborhood off Coming Street in Charleston. All my friends also had paper routes. The thing I didn't care for much was collecting for the paper which we did on Saturday mornings. That was often an entertaining experience at one barbershop I remember. I carried papers to the owner, who was a big jovial fellow, and he always used to kid me when I would come in collecting about the evils of 'the love of money.' It was as if he was prepping me for a reason not to pay or lenience to pay at another time. I figured that he had the best deal in town for the afternoon newspaper. All of his customers came in to read the paper whether they needed a haircut or not. But you couldn't help but like that man." Schachte related. "Charleston was like a large family. Everybody knew everybody."

The paper route triggered another fond memory.

"Once, I went to a lady's home, and her daughter came to the door and said, 'My mother said to tell you that she is not home.' So, I left and came back the following Saturday to try to collect. You'd get things like that. There was a lot of poverty across the community. The weekly fee of thirty cents was too much to pay for some." Schachte opined.

He added the other dynamics of having reliable and trusted friends.

"Freddy and Judy McMahon from across the street were always really close. Freddy is a year older than me. We used to get together, especially on Christmas Day. It was like we were a team of differing personalities growing up and fighting the odds together," Schachte reminisced. "Freddy and I would get together on our bicycles, and we would be out zooming around the neighborhood early—before first light."

The exuberance of youth in the simple times of a forgotten city provided many reflections.

"We lived at 152 Grove Street. Christmastime was always very special for me as an altar boy. I was always on the altar with many others for midnight Mass with Monsignor Wolfe, and he would give each altar boy a new and crisp $1 bill. One Christmas, he even gave me a book 'The Spirit of St. Louis'—which I read right away. It was the story of Charles Lindbergh's crossing the Atlantic. I was very appreciative of that and enjoyed the book immensely."

Schachte enumerated other childhood friendships—his cousins, and notable other relatives with pride. The personalities of that Grove Street neighborhood were memorable—in a childhood environment full of future achievers.

"My best friends were all, of course, from Charleston. I guess my neighborhood friends were always the closest. One of my best friends who is still close is retired United States Congressman Tommy Hartnett.

"I used to be a pretty good pitcher, and in fact, I threw a no-hitter during the Charleston playoffs in the Flea league. We used to play *Hartnett Real Estate*—his father's family business. I was always on the mound. It seemed that we always beat them, and Tommy to this day talks about that. We have remained great friends for a lifetime.

"Another best friend who is still in that category is Tommy Finnegan from that neighborhood. Dr. Tommy Finnegan retired as an orthodontist. We used to sell shoes at a local department store in the 1950s. Tommy is a couple of years older than me. He earned a dental degree after the award of a scholarship to Georgetown University in Washington. Tommy became a top orthodontist and among the most respected men of the community for his many kindnesses to others."

The Finnegan family is fully representative of Charleston's penchant for kindness and hospitality.

"In those early years, like my neighbors, I spent most of my time on the playground at Hampton Park which was within walking distance of my home on Grove Street. I was also in the Boy Scouts. Sacred Heart was the neighborhood parish. So much revolved around the old downtown parishes. As a former Eagle Scout and Scoutmaster who knew scouting and all the wholesome values it represented, we were proud of my dad. All the guys loved him, and they asked him questions about all matters because he was so worldly, giving, and knowledgeable."

"And of course, there was my cousin, Joe Riley," Schachte beamed with pride.

[Photo 9A] Joseph P. Riley, Jr., served as Mayor of Charleston for four decades. Photo by Author.

Joseph P. Riley, Jr., went on to be elected to the State of South Carolina legislature before serving as the mayor of Charleston for four decades (1975 to 2016).[15] Schachte's cousin Joe Riley is considered the catalyst visionary who changed Charleston to become a world travel destination and one of America's most livable cities. The cousins, the mayor and the admiral, were born nearly three years apart.

"I was always proud to be associated with Joe, Jr., who distinguished himself as a forty-year mayor. He has always been driven and dedicated. And he is and has been an exemplary Southern gentleman," Schachte stated. "Charleston wouldn't have become this current Charleston we enjoy without Joe Riley."

*Young Billy always looked up to his maternal grandfather.
Photo from Schachte family archives.*

"My mom and dad entertained dear friends. They had a vibrant supper club. In it were Joe Riley's mother and father. Their other supper club members were the Croghans and the Earhardts, along with a few other Charleston names that became well known. They would go to someone's home for drinks and then go out to eat at a local restaurant. There weren't too many local restaurants back in those days—only a handful. Because of my dad's work at the Charleston Navy Yard, it seems as though there was frequently a naval officer in our home. That fact became a subtle pathway to my career," Schachte explained. "My parent's guests left an impression upon me."

Christmas as well as other family seasonal gatherings included unique traditions.

"We often went down to the Schachte family home on Beaufain Street for a family get-together, where I saw my cousin Joe Riley's family. Joe's dad, Joe senior, was called 'Uncle Joe'—but he was a cousin and not an uncle." Schachte recalled the times. "Family was everything. Charleston's social footprint had been built upon the close-knit associations of friends—and especially family. It seemed like everybody knew everybody, and that sentiment extended well into the minority community, as well."

Schachte continued. "At these functions, they served Grandpa Schachte's punch to the grown-ups, which was extremely potent and a much-revered family receipt. The concoction was heavy on tea and heavier on bourbon and sugar." Schachte recalled. "I trust that the tradition and potency of that special tea-punch had been around even during the Prohibition years."

The family functions were a part of the calendar each and every year. The holiday season bore that standard.

"My Aunt Jree and her husband Gunnar would drive up from Beaufort where she was a teacher at the high school on the Paris Island Marine Corps Base. The Christmas gatherings were a special time for the extended family," Schachte added. "They wouldn't miss the festivities."

All channels of memories during those early years seemed to lead back to his father.

"Daddy's career rise was the stuff of storybooks. His intelligence advanced him often. He started as an electrician's helper, yet he ended up as the senior civilian employee in the Charleston Naval Shipyard. Any employee of the shipyard knew his name."

The Schachte family became a bastion of loyalty to the entire Charleston area.

"Daddy would never say it, but he had a role in key advancements because of his extraordinary abilities in his chosen field." Schachte informed. "He was considerably ahead of his time."

The Schachte family engendered a sense of community pride, coupled with expectations to excel academically and advance socially. Yet their demeanor was tempered by quiet humility.

The Schachtes extended their brand by a broad reach into Charleston's struggling community. The hundred-year decline since the end of the Civil War had taken its toll. The need for robust citizenry beckoned.

Young Billy Schachte was watching and listening.

"Once my mother told me that she sure hoped that one of her sons would become a naval officer someday. It's funny how those words left such a lasting impact. I think I was very young—only about ten years old. That stuck with me. I began to imagine being in the Navy uniform, and eventually, I pursued it into a full career." Schachte said. "The U.S. Navy's presence in Charleston was awesome."

The Schachtes earned their place in the culture of the Holy City. They were given nothing. Instead, they provided much. Unfortunately, a day would come when the Schachte world at Grove Street would suddenly transition.

"When my father died unexpectedly, my sisters got together and decided what we should put on his tombstone. It was simply the expression 'Loved by All.' That also pertained to my mother when she eventually passed away many years after my father. Daddy died on June 10, 1970. The youngest of us, brother Joe, had just finished high school." Schachte recalled. "It was an incredibly sad time."

His father's legacy remained well past his lifespan.

"Shortly after I retired from the Navy, I gave a speech at the Charleston Chapter of the Washington Light Infantry, and one of the fellas in the audience came up to me. He was in his mid to late 80's. He said he had worked with my father at the Shipyard, and that my dad had taught him something that he had taught his sons. I told him. 'I bet I knew what it was.'

"He asked, 'Well, what do you think it was?'"

"I answered that it was one of the first things my father taught me. It was to respect every man I meet because every man I meet likely knows more about some subject, item, or engineering matter than I did, so they deserve my respect regardless of their race or creed or station in life. That same message is what I tried to instill this in my sons, grandsons, and others," Schachte detailed.

"That older gentleman consented that my father taught him the very same lesson," the admiral confirmed.

The growing up years on Grove Street left a lasting impression on the future naval officer. He had the benefit of great parenting, a cohesive environment with his siblings, excellent friends, and the mentoring influences of his parents' friends.

CHAPTER 2
Upon Charleston Harbor

Growing up in a city that had mostly been forgotten in time was perhaps a blessing. Everyone seemed to know each other or know of each other. There was very little difference in household income levels.

"Everyone was, pretty much, in the same boat financially. The people that had the old historic mansions south of Broad Street had trouble maintaining them because it took too much caulk and paint and roofing repairs. They did what they could to keep the rain on the outside. The homes where we were on Grove Street were newer. Some dated from the early 1890s, others in the 1930s. Ours was built in 1939. The styles were similar. Those homes didn't need as many repairs," Schachte recalled. "We had small yards, but nobody hung around them that much. Hampton Park was just a couple of blocks away, next to College Park, our minor league baseball field. These were the wide-open spaces."

Charleston didn't have the ambiance that is much to its contemporary credit. New restaurants and hotels seem to open every other week in the newly popular destination city. But in the 1950s and 1960s, meals were seldom eaten elsewhere because there were so few restaurants.

Schachte explained, "We were lucky that my parents liked to cook things from scratch. They made spaghetti on Saturday with real chopped tomatoes and all the ingredients from a fresh market. It was the best. They made all the southern dishes that we now know were not-so-healthy. We had fried chicken, macaroni, red rice, ham, and every kind of potato dish. My dad would make other meaty dishes often enough."

The expectations of personal responsibility were an assumed rite of passage. Schachte found great mentorship at home and in the neighborhood. There were others at school he admired.

This 1947 photo shows the former Charleston Army Air Corps base, now the Joint Charleston Air Base. The three Schachte children enjoyed the ride to the country (then)—Kay, Margie, and Bill. Photo courtesy Schachte Family Archives.

"Beginning in my sophomore year in high school, I was mentored by a good priest who was on the faculty, Father Eddie Murphy. That was when I was thinking about going into the seminary. Father Murphy and I would get together occasionally after school to talk about things. He was indeed a very devout priest."

The priesthood and the convent were fundamental goals for those in Catholic education. It wasn't unusual for a large Catholic family to have multiple children dedicated to the life of service to the church. Because the Catholic Mass was traditionally performed in the Latin language of early Rome, most students subscribed to courses in Latin beginning in the 9th grade. Latin also formed a definitive basis for the study of other romantic languages, French, Spanish, and Italian. Word derivatives were merely interchangeable. A Latin scholar could access many other professions outside of the call to the cloth.

Schachte elaborated.

"My friends Dan Williman, Leland White, and Larry Duffy all went into the seminary from Bishop England High School. Dan went in early after his tenth-grade year. Leland and Larry went in after we graduated from high school. I think Larry stayed about a year after studying for a year in Rome. Some years later, Dan dropped out and got married. I saw him at our fiftieth high school class reunion. I suppose many thought me to be a cinch for the priesthood back then," Schachte reflected.

"The priests that taught at the high school were good men. They took an interest in helping students make adult decisions. They taught religion classes in addition to other core curriculum courses."

"At Bishop England High School, we studied the Old Testament for two years before getting into the New Testament. These teachers were priests and nuns—fine, highly educated scholars who taught us much about life outside of the courses. The high school experience was a wonderful and wholesome immersion into ethics and morality. My Bishop England High School diploma provided me a fine basis for a serious academic pursuit at nearly any college."

The first Catholic high school in South Carolina, Bishop England High School has produced many notable alumni in its century-plus history. In addition to Admiral Billy Schachte, those luminaries include S.C. First District U.S. Congressman Tommy Hartnett, actor Thomas Gibson, Miss Teen USA Vanessa Minnillo Lachey, forty-year Charleston Mayor Joseph P. Riley, Jr., best-selling author Dorothea Benton Frank, entrepreneur Michael Bennett, Federal District Judge P. Michael Duffy, and athletes Drew Meyer (baseball), Derek Hughes (football), and Temoc Suarez (soccer).

"The priests at Bishop England High School were demanding, but also fair and trusting. They rewarded good behavior and steady course work," he asserted. "Our education, especially in the faith, was paramount."

The youthful Schachte earned a friendship with an extraordinary priest who taught at the high school who would become the leading Catholic prelate in America.

"My first plane ride came to pass because of another influential member of the clergy. I had just turned fifteen, and Father Joseph Bernardin (pronounced *Burn-ar-dean*) asked me if I had ever had a plane ride before. I told him that I had not. He said he would like to provide a plane ride for me to Columbia on an errand to retrieve and to return to Charleston with his car. This excursion was a tremendous responsibility for me at that age.

"Father Bernardin owned a newer model Mercury two-door hardtop convertible that he had let some nuns borrow to return to their convent in Columbia. They were in Charleston for a special function and needed to get back to Columbia. Father Bernardin let them use his car to resolve the dilemma, though it left him with the issue of retrieving it. Of course, he checked with my father about me flying to Columbia to return his car."

Schachte continued to tell the story of his first airplane flight.

"The good priest showed up with a one-way plane ticket for me to fly from Charleston to Columbia. I was thrilled with the prospect of going on an airplane. The plane ride was amazing—a propeller plane. I loved the thrill of the take-off, having never been at that speed in anything before then," Schachte recalled. "All of my friends were jealous. Nobody had the financial wherewithal to travel on an airplane back then. I had the experience of a lifetime that day. It was as if on that one day, I became worldly because I had been on an airplane to Columbia."

He described the return.

"The nuns met me at the airport, and I rode with them back to their convent. Then, I took off with his beautiful Mercury. In later life, I reflected on that and was amazed at how much trust Father Bernardin had in me—a young fifteen-year-old boy. I drove his new car the 110-mile trip from Columbia to Charleston before the days of interstate highways. I got to his rectory, and he gave me a ride to my home on Grove Street. I thanked him again for what he may have considered as a favor to him. It was much more of an unforgettable adventure to me," Schachte stated. "And I had not had a driver's license that long."

Years later, Joseph Louis Cardinal Bernardin became the highest-ranking Catholic clergyman in the United States.[16] He was considered a serious potential successor to Pope Paul II. Cardinal Bernardin was born in Columbia, South Carolina, in 1928 and died in Chicago of pancreatic cancer in 1996.[17] No United States Cardinal ever received as much consideration for the papacy.

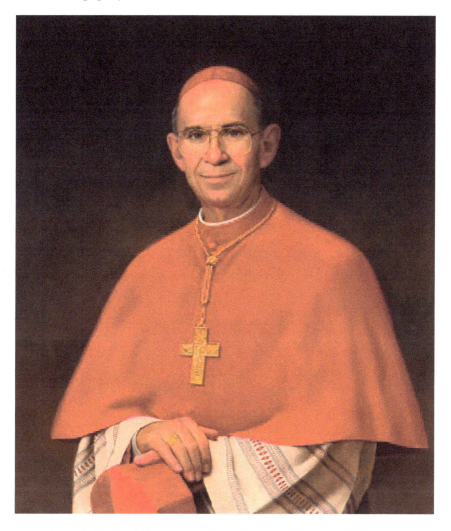

Joseph Cardinal Bernardin. Photo Courtesy Diocese of Chicago.

As his Bishop England High School experiences fortified his academic prowess, a college choice beckoned. The Catholic Seminary was still a possibility. Schachte vacillated over the sentiment to become a Catholic Priest. Having a girlfriend at the time was a substantial dilemma.

"Looking back, having a girlfriend in high school was incompatible with becoming a Catholic Priest. I decided not to pursue the cloth. It was a very tough decision. I especially admired those who elevated themselves to a religious calling.

"I applied to Clemson University, which was no surprise to anyone who knew me then. Looking back, I made a reasonable choice between the priesthood and the pursuit of a traditional future marriage because I later found my lovely wife, Carmen. Carmen became my greatest asset."

There were no alternative plans fully discussed with his father about college. It was assumed—a given—that he would be attending the same college as his father and his grandfather. Clemson University was a Schachte tradition. But late in high school, Schachte had a sense that he might part with that educational destination.

"Clemson won out, but when it came time to go to college, I had already taken a pre-seminary physical. And the influence was strong because several of my best friends in high school had gone into the seminary. So, I was comfortable with the seminary option," Schachte confided. "But in the end, I made the proper choice."

The time to leave the comfort of family life on Grove Street had arrived. So many of his neighborhood friends had scattered down different avenues to adult life.

Schachte headed for Clemson in 1958. More responsibilities and the intention of career success expected by his diligent parents propelled a result. The young Charlestonian was determined to advance and flourish.

*Kay, Bill, Marjorie, and Frank circa 1947.
Photo courtesy of Schachte Family Archives.*

CHAPTER 3

The Clemson Years

"Choosing Clemson was normal for me. The pedigree of my father and grandfather earning electrical engineering degrees there was a strong indicator. As it turned out, my Clemson education was the right path. Our oldest son, Billy, went there as well and graduated in 1989. Each of us was named William Leon Schachte.

"I am a junior. My son, Billy, was named the third. My dad was a junior until his father passed away in the 1930s. So, he dropped the junior. Daddy probably confused the census-takers and the family heritage sites on the Internet."

Schachte's Clemson experience created warm memories.

"Clemson was a land grant college which required all incoming students to spend two years in an ROTC program. I chose the Air Force basically because they did not drill with rifles. I completed my two years, and that was it for the ROTC," Schachte recalled.

A Pennsylvanian, Thomas Green Clemson, married John C. Calhoun's daughter, Anna Maria, and moved to her father's family plantation near Anderson, SC.[18] Maria's father was the Vice President of the United States under two different presidents from 1825 to 1832. [19]

An agronomist and engineer, Thomas Clemson left his considerable fortune to the State of South Carolina with intentions to build an upstate college specializing in agriculture. The campus opened in 1893[20] with less than 500 students as a military, male-only, white-only institution. Clemson Agricultural College enjoyed many successes, and notably hired John Heisman to coach the Tigers' early football program (1900-1903). The annual Heisman Trophy award, emblematic as college football's best player, was named for the legendary coach.[21]

In 1955, Clemson transitioned to a civilian co-educational college.[22] Just eight years later, with the then-controversial admission of Harvey Gantt, Clemson became the first institution in the state to fully embrace integration.[23] The college transitioned to university status the next year, 1964.[24] Though founded as an agricultural and military college, the institution's emphasis evolved to myriad academic pursuits, most notably their vaunted programs of research and engineering.[25]

"Clemson at that time was transitioning into what became a university. The majors were heavy in engineering and sciences, and the courses reflected that. I had to take several engineering-type courses, although I wanted to be a pre-law major. They didn't have such a program. So, I majored in English and minored in History. I eventually got through physics and the other engineering-type courses. I enjoyed English and History and did pretty well in my major and minor programs," he recalled.

There were other avenues of activity at the somewhat-remote college.

"I had always been active—starting with my time at Boys State as a rising senior at Bishop England High School. Both Larry Duffy and Leland White were also chosen to attend. When I got to Clemson, I realized that there were some students in the freshman class that I had met at Boys State. I ran for class president of the freshman class and was elected. The next year I ran for president of the sophomore class and was again elected to that position," Schachte reflected.

"I recall my father telling great stories of the collegiality and comradeship as part of the Clemson Corps of Cadets. Some friends of mine and I got interested in the fraternity experience. Accordingly, we formed a fraternity, and we were the first social fraternity ever authorized on campus at Clemson. At the time, we were called Sigma Alpha Zeta (SAZ). I was later elected president of that fraternity, and I was also elected the first president of the first Inter-Fraternity Council at Clemson. It seems that I did everything but study. I was also the vice-president of the organization known as the Tiger Brotherhood. I was president of the Clemson Student Senate and a senator and then-governor of the South Carolina State Student Legislature.

My hat's off to all the colleges in South Carolina who would elect representatives and senators to understand our system at the State House better. These elected students would then vote for the Executive Branch—the governor and lieutenant governor. They took everyone to the State House and Senate office building in Columbia. It was an exceptional and insightful experience," he recalled.

Schachte served ably as his Clemson University class president. He embraced leadership as a duty. His interest was to speak independently of his values but forcefully about fairness. He had a solid basis for the societal insights that would later define his life.

"That brave African-American student, Harvey Gantt, transferred from the University of Iowa in January of 1963," Schachte reflected. "It would be a transformational time. I felt for Gantt's difficult plight."

Harvey Gantt later distinguished himself as the first African-American mayor of Charlotte, North Carolina.[26] But getting into a previously all-white student population in the times that mirrored societal upheavals had to be daunting—if not threatening of physical violence. Clemson had the potential to become a confrontational battleground. Utilizing his leadership role at the college, Schachte embraced the timely and needed cultural transition.

Center of Clemson University Campus, the "Main Building" from this 1903 photograph, it was renamed Tillman Hall in 1946 for former South Carolina Governor Benjamin Tillman. Photo Courtesy SC SciWay.

"I reacted based on the fairness taught in my home. Harvey Gantt had every right to enter Clemson, and I was outspoken in my support." Schachte backed up the sentiment by published quotes he gave to the media at the time.

"We integrated Clemson with the admittance of Harvey Gantt. The press was all over campus at that time. Several of us who were deemed to be student leaders got together at the request of the media for questions. An Associated Press reporter was there. The story that he wrote went across the U.S. media wires. An A.P. article that appeared in local papers, as well as *Newsweek* and *Time Magazine, quoted me*," Schachte recalled the controversy.

"It reported, 'Bill Schachte, a former governor of South Carolina State Student Legislature, of Charleston said, 'the inevitable has finally reached South Carolina. I am glad that Clemson has been called upon to shoulder the responsibility of changing times. Most of us despise the portrait of Uncle Sam standing before the world with Mississippi mud in his face.'

The quote was appropriate and helped to usher in a new era in the South.

"As you can imagine, not all agreed with my point of view. But I knew that admitting Harvey Gantt to Clemson was the right step forward—not only at Clemson but for our country."

Transfer student Harvey Gantt leaves the registrar's office at Clemson. Photo courtesy of Clemson University.

The Harvey Gantt story enthused some, confused some, and angered others. But the event was handled properly and without incident. Gantt's later political career became a point of pride with the Clemson faithful. Gantt found a solid advocate in the form of senior student leadership— Billy Schachte.

Schachte continued to excel in his academic pursuits while remaining active in campus life. He built a legacy at the tucked-away institution of progress.

"The whole experience at Clemson was nothing short of exceptional," Schachte related.

"Like any typical college fraternity guy, I had several close friends. Having been a politically active student, I was blessed by many other dear friends. At the top of that list was Allen Wood, an architecture major from Florence, S.C. Allen and I used to wait on tables at the Clemson House Hotel Banquet Hall. The waiters were also provided supper before our shift time started. Allen and I had a good time working that job together. He also came from an interesting background."

The relationship he enjoyed with his good friend Allen Wood would relate to another important time in Schachte's lifetime of achievement.

"After graduating, Allen became a very successful architect in Florence." Schachte said. "We would typically see each other on occasions, especially when Carmen and I were on campus to attend a home football game. Fast forward some years, and Allen was on the Board of Trustees at Clemson— later serving for several years as its chairman. I was then a two-star admiral and in command of the Navy Legal Service Offices.

"Accordingly, I would hold regional meetings to meet with my commanding officers. One such meeting for our Southeast Region was in Charleston. I was staying at the Base BOQ (Bachelor Officer's Quarters). When I arrived to start that session at 8:00 a.m., I walked to the podium and was shocked to see my mother sitting on the front row. I started the meeting by welcoming the surprise guest and then noticed in the back of the room was my dear friend Allen Wood. As it turned out, Allen was there on behalf of the governor as a last-minute substitute to make a presentation. I received *The Order of the Palmetto*. He drove down from Florence the night before to be at the 8:00 meeting. He then made that surprise presentation. It startled me. I had no idea it was coming. My mother later remarked that she had never seen me like that—speechless!"

The Order of the Palmetto is the highest award conferred upon a citizen of the State of South Carolina. The sitting governor of the state traditionally awards it.[27]

Schachte had come a long way from his Clemson roots. He knew much of what to expect at the hamlet setting where Georgia and North Carolina squeeze the top of his home state. His father had walked the magnolia-treed lanes there before him, as did his dad's dad. The admiral would return, years later. The college had called him back to honor him, as well.

"In 1999, Clemson University President Constantine W. 'Dino' Curris called me to inform me that the faculty and Board of Trustees had voted to award me one of the two Honorary Doctorate Degrees. The prestigious award was made at that May graduation ceremony with Allen Wood sitting on the stage as a board trustee. I assume he was the initiating influence of that honor." Schachte offered. "My friendship with the once-orphaned aspiring architect Allen Wood came full circle."

Schachte's years at Clemson had other experiences that impacted his career and viewpoint. There were also times to stand up and be accountable. Schachte did this when it was not popular to do so in the deep south. But he knew what was right.

He summed up the relationships he fostered and maintained while at Clemson.

"When I graduated, I was named as one of sixteen 'Outstanding Seniors' selected by my classmates. The selection was 'based on extra-curricular activities, leadership, publications, athletics, intelligence, personality, versatility, fellowship, and character.' I was honored by that selection and yet humbled that my classmates were so kind and considerate. I was proud to be a member of the Clemson Class of 1963."

His graduation was an entry to a rapidly changing world. The Vietnam conflict had grown into nightly news stories laced with morbidity. It was halfway around the globe but closely monitored in the consciousness of every draft-eligible male in America. The intersection of that far-away war competed for headlines with the Civil Rights movement at home and the emergence of admirable leaders such as Martin Luther King. On November 22nd of that year, President John Fitzgerald Kennedy assassination in Dallas shocked the world.

There was turbulence ahead. Schachte's tranquil seas were turning into swells and then storms.

CHAPTER 4
The Navy Option

"Upon graduation from Clemson, my dad got a call from a friend who was on the Draft Board reminding him that his son Billy—me—had no more deferments. I had graduated from college and was not married. I was going to be drafted. I anticipated that possibility.

"I took advice well, and right away, I drove to Columbia and spent the night at the home of a fraternity brother's family. The next day I took the test for Officers Candidate School at the U.S. Navy recruiting station in downtown Columbia. Fortunately, I passed the OCS exam. The Navy officer administering the test informed me that I had passed—and if I wanted to—he could swear me into the Navy right then and there. I agreed with that and raised my hand, and I was immediately sworn into the United States Navy. I got back home, and two days later, I had a draft notice from the United States Army—so my timing was fortunate.

Schachte attended Officers Candidate School Training in Newport, Rhode Island. The experience was both challenging and fulfilling. The new ensign would report ready for service by his post-school naval assignment.

"After graduating from OCS, I requested a small ship and was promptly assigned to the *Lorain County*.[28] This ship was an LST (Landing Ship Tank) which as stationed in Little Creek near the Norfolk, Virginia area. I really enjoyed my time on the Lorain County," Schachte recalled. "It was my indoctrination into the life of a sailor."

The Lorain County was named for a county in Ohio.[29] The ship took part in the Cuban Missile Crisis blockade of 1962. The Lorain County served the U.S. Navy until 2002.[30]

It was during his service on the Lorain County that Billy Schachte met and married the bright and attractive Carmen Figueroa. The formal wedding was in her hometown in Puerto Rico. Though stationed in Virginia, the newlyweds would find the meanderings of world politic to be their destiny. The early years were navy-normal with training, maneuvers, and at-sea duties.

In eighteen months, Schachte earned the designation of lieutenant junior grade. The idea of a career in the Navy was coming into focus, but not certain.

"When you're young, and the whole world seems to be ahead of you, you have to find your own way. I was not sure that the Navy would be my career, but it certainly provided me with a viable and adventurous option," Schachte remembered. "Carmen and I never knew what would be coming next, and generally accepted that the career path was promising enough to follow."

USS Lorain County Photo Courtesy U.S. Navy Archives

"I never considered myself a 'lifer.' After being onboard for about a month, I was able to go home to Charleston for a one-week leave. On returning to the ship, I found out I had been volunteered by the commanding officer to attend what was called a Junior Officer Leadership Training Course at the Amphibious Base at Little Creek (Virginia). It was a part of the UDT (Underwater Demolition Team) training. The UDT eventually became the Navy SEALS," Schachte explained.

His Navy experiences were destined to broaden. He was ready for the experience, though with some trepidation.

"Admiral McCain, the commander of Amphibious Forces Atlantic, was told by the budget people that he was going to have to drop the last session of that UDT Training to save some money. McCain disregarded that suggestion and decided to keep that portion of the training going and call it a Junior Officer Leadership Training Course. One other person on my ship was assigned," Schachte related. "Admiral McCain was the right guy for the job. He knew we needed this type of Navy specialist training."

Admiral John Sidney McCain Jr. retired as a four-star admiral in 1972.[31] He had become the first full admiral in the history of the Navy who was the son of a full admiral (John S. McCain, Sr., 1884-1945).[32] The junior McCain's son, John III, became a prisoner of war, a presidential candidate (2008) and the United States Senator from Arizona. He died in 2018.[33]

"We were assigned to the base at Little Creek, where we experienced hand-to-hand combat training. Then they put us through some other rigorous courses. We were assigned for intense escape and evasion training. Our instructors were led by an LDO (a limited duty officer). This very memorable officer was a fine former Marine and a pure-blooded Native American. He got your attention! We were put in the back of a covered truck and driven north to the A.P. Hill Army Base Camp."

Schachte continued to tell of the intentionally-taxing training experience.

"We were instructed and given a compass, a map. We had to reach rendezvous points by avoiding capture. I was fortunate. My group consisted of two other ensigns—one of whom had been an Eagle Scout and was very familiar with what we were about to do. Another ensign was a civil engineering officer," he recalled. "I had a good team with wide abilities. The three of us worked very well together."

He recalled the conditions and the planned depravity.

"At the beginning of the training, those of us who smoked were allowed to take three cigarettes. Not knowing what was about to happen, I also put a five-dollar bill inside my boot sock. I didn't know what good that would do, but I did it anyway. And off we went for three days. Each person was also given a potato, and we were supposed to survive off things we could find on the land. We planned it out amongst ourselves with some solid survival strategies. We had several close calls, but we were never captured. Not getting captured meant that you beat the odds and survived," Schachte related the experience. "It meant that we passed the worst of it."

He spoke about the evasive maneuvers that the threesome of ensigns utilized.

"We were doing things like walking backward as we moved across dirt roads. Simultaneously, there was an Army bivouac going on—a bunch of tanks—and we were avoiding them and making sure we were doing the little things we could to evade detection," Schachte retold the experience. "We were determined."

Schachte smiled at a part of the memory.

"The other two ensigns got upset with me because I smoked my three cigarettes in the first hour and—as we were trying to get to sleep at night—I would suggest food thoughts to them. I'd say things like, 'Do you remember what it would taste like to have a nice thick chocolate milkshake and a nice juicy hamburger?' Well, of course, they didn't like that mental picture while we were in that grueling adventure. We were famished—with pangs of hunger. Hunger can dominate your thinking and disrupt your judgment.

"They'd say, 'Shut up, Bill. Let's get some shut-eye.' But I had my reasons—and I knew if we succeeded that my five-dollar bill would make the survival experience quite memorable."

He continued to tell of the survival experience.

"As it turned out after two days of outstanding teamwork in our evasive maneuvers—and not getting captured—some helicopters showed up, and we were told that our session had been canceled. It was because one of our teams had been lost in the expanse of terrain. They couldn't find those guys. So, they got us to go to a rendezvous point by a waterfall. There, they passed out soap and told us to take a shower, and they would get back to us. We were instructed just to take it easy. That's an order you like to hear," Schachte smiled. "I had that five-dollar bill and a plan."

I mentioned to my two buddies that I saw a couple of gas stations as we were leaving the interstate two days earlier. Back in those days, 1964, they also sold beer in these out-of-the-way stations. So, I told the other two guys, 'Let's go out and hitch-hike and get to one of those gas stations. They didn't tell us we couldn't leave. They just told us to take it easy and relax—and they'd be back to get us. So, heading off to get a beer was within the instructions, I rationalized."

Schachte led the two ensigns to the highway.

"We caught a ride to a gas station. We got in there, and I whipped out my five dollars and bought my two pals a round of beer. At about the time that we were standing there, drinking that cold beer as a victory salute, the searchers had found the lost team. Two jeeps pulled up outside and the head of the program, this lieutenant commander—the same former Native American Marine fellow—came in to have some beer. They saw us standing there."

Schachte recounted the loud and confrontational experience.

"They were upset, and they ordered us to get in one of the jeeps. They drove us back to the camp. They did admit that we didn't do anything wrong. We were not told any instructions, for instance—not to rendezvous at a gas station for beer. Looking back, I think it was an exceptional idea," Schachte intimated. "But we were reminded in loud tones that it was not what they meant."

"The commanding officers were delighted that they had found the lost group, and there were no injuries. They had no other major concern when it was all over," Schachte stated. "We had acted independently. I suppose it's not okay to buy a beer for your friends from hidden money in your boot when you're supposed to be in a difficult training exercise. Really, I think they were angry because we had beaten the system and celebrated."

Schachte smiled at the memory. He had defeated the constancy of fatigue and hunger with remarkable teammates who used guile and instinct to evade capture. The UDT Training that was the forerunner of the Navy Seal program would become consequential in Schachte's later career.

"To be sure, there was much more to the program than hand-to-hand combat and evading enemy capture. The program was comprehensive and life-changing." Schachte remarked. "I learned valuable lessons that I applied to the rest of my life."

The Newport News Area of Virginia. Photo courtesy of United States Navy.

Schachte recalled a postscript. "Fast forward some three years, and I was in Swift Boat training in Coronado, California. The Navy had an escape and evasion phase for this as well. I told the instructor I already had that training. They checked my records and reported that there was no record of it.

"I further inquired about the training that was going on in California and was informed that it was headed by an LDO (limited duty officer), a commander at that time, who was a full-blooded Native American. I realized that this could be the same trainer from the Virginia experience. What were the chances? His reputation was that he was very adept in surviving in jungle environments and he was a rugged commando-type. He was most qualified to head that phase of the program," Schachte stated. "He was 'one tough hombre,' as they say."

Schachte realized that since the records were not updated, he might have to go through the evasion-of-capture phase again.

"I believed that there was a chance that I could be excused since it was a course I had previously completed successfully. The records of his training completion had not surfaced. Schachte had one other avenue to prove that he should be excused from the repetition.

"I remembered that the beer rendezvous story would likely remind the trainer of my participation a few years before—if this were the same Native American trainer. I told them that story about the beer, getting caught at the gas station, and although there was nothing in my record, I thought that maybe the Native American training specialist might remember me because of the loud confrontation when they found us in that gas station drinking that cold beer. By my good fortune, it was indeed the same former Marine officer from the beer story. And he did remember me—vaguely.

"The commander's verbal report was repeated back to me. He couldn't remember exactly what my name was—but it that it started with an 'S' and was German-sounding—and that my first name was 'Bill' and that I was an ensign at the time. The people in charge of the school informed me that I did not have to go through that training since I had emerged from the other session successfully—never captured. The records were corrected."

The Schachte name is not German, but Prussian. Prussia contained lands on the southern shores of the Baltic Sea into present Germany and across to western Poland. It was a monarchy that existed between 1701 and 1918.[34] Famous Prussians include Paul von Hindenburg, Kaiser Wilhelm, and Otto von Bismarck. The Prussian General Friedrich Wilhelm von Steuben was quite consequential to the American Revolution related to his role as a military tactician and drillmaster for the Continental Army.[35] The Prussian-born Schachtes emigrated to the United States in the 1800s before their ancestral home country became a footnote of history. The European maps changed.

"A Prussian name would be accurate, but there is no longer a Prussia," Schachte detailed.

The admiral continued retelling the "small world" episode of his California Swift Boat training. He had gained a few extra free days unexpectedly and would devote them to family time. His rendezvous was with his wife, Carmen.

"One of the future Swift Boat skippers was a friend of mine who I had met in the course of the training, and he knew that I was excused. So, he let me borrow his car. I had no car at that time. This break gave me time to spend with Carmen and little Billy. Billy was just a little tiny guy and had just learned to walk back then.

"A few days later, I brought the car back to meet those fellows when they returned from the grueling training. They were all huddled in a big truck, and all needed a shave. It made me remember how I felt when I did that phase a few years earlier—tired, hungry, and scruffy. But they were not too happy to see this fellow officer, clean-shaven with his wife waiting on them in the parking lot. What could I say? I just smiled," Schachte responded. "After all, I had already passed that test."

"They were good guys, and it worked out well. But I'm not sure all of them knew the story that I had already passed the training previously." Schachte recalled.

Schachte was promoted to Navy Lieutenant. He still had no plan of certainty to remain in the Navy for a career though a career was the leading option. It was not the conclusive option.

"It's funny how converging circumstances change a life," Schachte offered. "I knew that I had compatriots who had made the courageous step to volunteer for the Southeast Asian theater. I sensed that I needed to do the same to fulfill my commitment to the Navy and the country. Vietnam was very real. I felt that to serve in the military was an honor and a privilege, but to serve where most needed was the true calling of the military."

His plan for the immediate future would be brazen. And he knew that that plan would upset his young wife, Carmen. His conviction was that his military service was to be full and meaningful—whether a shorter stint or a longer one—was to matter. He made a bold decision.

"I made the choice to volunteer for Vietnam. I felt that I was ready and that the training had prepared me well. But one can never assimilate war. I stepped forward and made up my mind to engage in the conflict that lingered over every service person's shoulder. My hardest duty after that was not so much to serve that commitment but to sit down and explain my decision to Carmen. We had been married for only three years." Schachte retold. "And finding someone like Carmen was my greatest achievement in life. She loved me enough to let me serve in the way I felt most fulfilling to my character and sense of patriotism."

The Vietnam decision was another in his lifetime sequence of unlikelihoods for Schachte. It was just three years earlier that their marriage hinged on a letter from his Charleston pastor attesting to his character and eligibility to be married in the Catholic Church. Without that, the courtship and marriage to Carmen may have never happened.

Through it all, he hoped to emerge fulfilled in his commitment to his country and completed in his dedication to his lifelong companion whom he loved dearly.

CHAPTER 5
Carmen for a Lifetime

The warmth of the courtship and marriage to Carmen Figueroa went beyond the storybook sunshine of a Caribbean island. Schachte recalled the sequence, the obstacles, and the traditional asking of her hand in marriage.

"While assigned to the Lorain County, I left the Virginia base with an amphibious ready group. We had a battalion of Marines spread out among several ships and brought them down to Panama where they underwent jungle warfare training. At about the same time, the political situation in the Dominican Republic was heating up."

By 1965, there were political tensions in Santo Domingo, the capital of the Dominican Republic. The fear of instability in the island republic became the basis of U.S. President Lyndon Johnson's decision to send troops. As Johnson stated publicly, he "did not want a second Cuba in the Caribbean."[36]

"When we came back to the States, we docked at Little Creek in the Norfolk area. We had stops in Jamaica and then several stops in Puerto Rico.

It was on our first stop in Puerto Rico that I met an incredible and beautiful person who—as it turned out—was to be my wife.

Carmen Figueroa grew upon Ceiba, a town just an hour's ride from the capital of San Juan. Ceiba is near Fajardo, the home of the former U.S. Navy Base at Roosevelt Roads--where Schachte and his ship, the *Lorain County*, had docked. The couple would need a serendipitous occasion to meet.

"We were restricted to the base because of the Dominican Republic situation, and we were all on a pretty involved 'stand-by' assignment. Eventually, we had some free time to go to the Officer's Club. I was with my roommate, Ted Jones. To our delight, there were several ladies in the club. I later found out that the admiral's wife had instituted a program to give base passes to girls who lived in the area. These young ladies all came from fine and respectful local families. All were college graduates. Carmen was among that group that evening," Schachte recalled. "We were all elated to have those ladies visiting the O-Club."

There was music and an air of festivity. The young naval officers were elated to host the pretty visitors.

"The first person to spot her was Ted, my roommate, because Carmen was laughing at someone else's joke. It was just enchanting to hear her voice even then. So, Ted went over and danced with her and then I danced with her a couple of times. She was a delightful person from those very first moments. Before leaving, I invited her and her friend, Hilda Moreno, to join us in the wardroom for lunch the next day," Schachte retold. "That was a unique privilege we had as officers."

The next day, the ladies had courteously responded. They came for lunch.

"My ship was in port, not too far from where the Officer's Club was located. So, the next morning, I was outside standing the quarterdeck watch in the LST, and the bow ramp was down, and the bow doors were open.

"One of the enlisted men came over to me and said, 'Mr. Schachte, sir, look out at the parking lot there in front of the ship. There is a car with two really cute girls, and they keep looking at the ship.'

"These were the young ladies that I had invited for lunch in the wardroom. I was unsure that they would accept. So, I quickly got on the phone that was on the quarterdeck and cranked up the wardroom. I told the head steward to put two more plates out and tell the Captain I would explain later. Carmen and Hilda joined us for lunch on the ship, and it was very enlightening. They were both well-educated and interesting guests. We found that they had recently traveled throughout Europe. They had insightful stories to tell about that travel experience."

Schachte continued to tell the story of his keen interest in Carmen.

"I decided to show Carmen around the ship after lunch. I brought her up to show her my stateroom that I shared with Ted. We were prepared for sea, so my personal desk was locked up. The top writing area was secured for foul weather. I opened it to show it to Carmen, and there was a picture of two women there. Well, one was a cute young blonde-haired girl, my goddaughter, Julie Cozy. This was my sister Kay's youngest daughter, my niece. The other photo was a picture of my mother.

I later found out Carmen was convinced that the little girl was my daughter. She likely thought I was a fraud," Schachte recalled. "But I did not know that at the time."

Despite the suspicions, the young miss was gracious and cordial to the Navy ensign.

"We had a grand time, and Carmen left. We were still restricted to the base because of the Dominican Republic situation.

"The next day I was scheduled to go to San Juan to take a team of people—both enlisted and officers—to grade an exercise. We called it the 'man overboard at sea.' The exercise was aboard the USS Plymouth Rock, an LSD (dock landing ship). We utilized the Plymouth Rock because it was a larger ship than the Lorain County and suited the exercise better.

"We headed to San Juan from the base at Roosevelt Roads. It was a four-lane highway, and this car came by, and one of the enlisted guys in my car said, 'My God, did you see all the women in that car!' I said, 'No, I really had not noticed.' I was intrigued, so I got a little closer. Sure enough, it was a car full of women. I flashed the lights, and the car pulled over. The person who was driving got out of the car. Incredibly, that person was Carmen. She was teaching in the Puerto Rican School Systems, and she had several other schoolteachers in the car driving them to San Juan for some kind of a teacher's conference," Schachte recalled. "What were the chances of us meeting on that highway the very next day after she visited the ship? I suppose it was fate."

The stars were aligned.

"Carmen laughed at seeing me again. I thought this to be an opportune time to ask her out. So, we agreed to have a date that same evening. We started dating, and before I knew it, the relationship became very serious on my part—and then on hers, as well. In time, my ship had to leave to return to the States. There would be some more maneuvering with the ships involved with the Dominican Republic situation. That political situation was getting intense and then cooling down," Schachte recalled.

Caribbean political upheaval paved the way for an unlikely romance.

"In time, I had gotten very serious about this incredibly wonderful person I had met named Carmen. However, her doting father in Puerto Rico would not have anything to do with me. Mr. Figueroa was deeply suspicious of the Navy and the sailors that arrived in the Ceiba area. There had been some history there, perhaps, that had fueled his concerns. Once the relationship became serious, Carmen's father required that I produce a letter signed by my pastor at my Catholic church in Charleston--on the church letterhead stationery--stating that I was a practicing Catholic," Schachte detailed. "He further wanted to verify that I was not married at the time, that I had never been married, and that I came from a nice family. He was very protective of his beautiful daughter. And you really couldn't blame him for that."

The love-struck naval officer returned to the States. Schachte had adequate general leave time to travel back to Charleston to visit his family. It was essential to alleviate the concerns of Carmen's father.

"I went to see Monsignor Manning with my father after I came back down from Norfolk to Charleston. We had a nice meeting. Monsignor Manning got a kick out of the strange request from a doting father on Puerto Rico. But he did, in fact, write the letter and mailed it to Carmen's pastor at their Ceiba church to be delivered to Mr. Figueroa."

He recalled the process and the result. The verification process of a naval officer's credentials, character, and creed were most unusual but worth the extra effort.

"I later heard from Carmen that her father said it was alright for me, if I were coming to Puerto Rico, to visit the Figueroa family. This was a serious matter. I had been unable to do that before then. I took advantage of the invitation.

"When I returned, I found that her family was delightful--but very formal and protective. They were close-knit. But seeing that gave me a positive impression of the Figueroa family," Schachte found. "Carmen and I began to see each other with their blessing."

"So, one thing led to another in the courtship process, and I wrote to her father asking for her hand and marriage. He agreed because he had gotten that initial letter and had come to know me and my intentions as sincere," Schachte said. "This was a major point in his life, as well."

The formality was necessary and made the experience all the more charming.

"Mr. Figueroa did tell me that Carmen was the only daughter in the family. She had three brothers. But he said she had been acting a little differently. He could tell that something was going on in her life. The offer of my visits was extended. I did so. I was still stationed in Little Creek, Virginia. This was a by-chance, long-distance relationship," he added.

Schachte retraced the events.

"Carmen and I decided to get married sooner than later. We didn't want to wait. The Navy had this problem with the Dominican Republic going on all the while. Accordingly, we set a date for the wedding on the 20th of May 1965. Unfortunately, that happened to be a Thursday. I only had one extra day for the honeymoon before I had to get back to the ship in Little Creek.

"By circumstance, and for a short period, my two sisters and their children were living at home with my parents. Nonetheless, my father was able to break away to be my best man at the wedding in Puerto Rico. When he arrived, it was so reassuring to me, and he was really very happy that he met Carmen's family. Actually, the priest that was their pastor also said some very nice things about her family," Schachte recounted.

The Figueroa family traditions and their closeness mirrored that of the Schachtes in Charleston. This sense of unity gave confidence to Schachte's father that Carmen had been brought up in a healthy and religious family environment.

"Since we were having a full Catholic Nuptial Mass, I had to go to confession in order to receive communion. The pastor knew of a young priest in a neighboring city, Fajardo, who agreed to meet with me and hear my confession. I went over and met with this priest. He was a young fellow. He was very spiritual and a handsome priest. He heard my confession, and I guess we really hit it off. He said, 'I would really like to attend your wedding. Do you think you could arrange that?'

"I replied, 'Absolutely.' We made sure that he was invited.

"The wedding was partially filmed, somewhat rare for 1965. In the old video reel, you can see this young priest on the altar with us," Schachte explained. "I think he genuinely enjoyed being there."

Schachte further described the details of that special day.

"My dad served as my best man—and that was personally reassuring to me. He gave me a piece of fatherly advice. He told me that--on the day of the wedding--not to have a drop of alcohol until the reception. I honored the advice. We had a grand time, and the wedding was beautiful. Everything turned out well. When we got to the Officer's Club for the reception, Dad brought me a double-bourbon and ginger ale. He was a great best man! Everybody started dancing and getting into a festive mood, although it was on a Thursday—not a weekend festivity. The next thing I knew, Dad was up on the stage with the saxophone returning to his days at Clemson, where he led that old band from the 1930s--the 'Jungleers.' He was fantastic. There never seemed to be an end to his talent," Schachte reflected.

The Schachte-Figueroa wedding in 1965.
"I married the most wonderful girl I ever met!"

It was a wedding of great joy for the fine Puerto Rican hosts.

"They loved my father. He was so outgoing and entertaining. People were coming up to Carmen, telling her if his son is anything like the father, she will indeed have an enchanted life. That part was true about my father—everybody loved Daddy. We had two bands playing at the wedding. One was a traditional Caribbean steel drum band. Dad could play the steel drums. He entertained the crowd until late into the evening. I was so proud to be his son," Schachte reminisced.

"We returned to the El Conquistador where Carmen and I had our one-night honeymoon. We got up the next morning and went down to the beach on a funicular[37], and then we went back and retrieved Daddy to get him to the airport and back to Charleston. He had already been promoted to become the number one civilian employee at the Charleston Navy Shipyard by then," Schachte recalled.

The wedding and short honeymoon went by all-too-quickly.

"When Daddy met my brother Frank in the airport in Charlotte where he flew direct from San Juan, he had time to tell him about the wedding. Frank was a student at nearby Belmont Abbey College near Charlotte. Frank and some of his friends went to a restaurant at the airport and were having some beer with Daddy before he had to catch the next flight to Charleston. Frank told me about the conversation.

First home quarters in Norfolk, Virginia
Photo courtesy of Schachte family archives.

"Daddy told them all about the wedding and Carmen and her family. Frank related to me that Daddy was just so excited. The waitress came over and said, 'I'm sorry sir, but if you are going to be drinking alcohol you have to have a meal here. So, Daddy ordered a round of french fries for everybody and a bottle of champagne. Then he said something that made all the difference in the world to me. He told Frank and the rest of them that my wife, Carmen, reminded him most of my Aunt Marie. He could not have said anything more spectacular than that."

Schachte further explained the reference to his Aunt Marie.

"My Uncle Henry's wife, my Aunt Marie, was like a queen among all of us. She was just a spectacular person. She was a nurse, and she was both beautiful and elegant. We all adored her," he recounted. "Daddy could not have described Carmen to my brother any better. And that description was repeated when he got back to the family in Charleston."

The life of a married naval officer would be challenging. Carmen fully understood the chosen path.

"I had to get back to the ship in Virginia from Puerto Rico—now married with a wonderful new bride who would be leaving her family. I'm sure that this was an exciting--yet sentimental--time for Carmen," Schachte retold. "It had to be hard for her."

"Carmen and I got back to Norfolk, and we moved into government quarters at the Naval Air Station. They had quarters for young married couples, and it was just a marvelous time in our lives.

"I had a two-seater Fiat convertible roadster—not much of a family car—and I started having car trouble. I needed to be getting back and forth to the ship. I did the smart mature thing," Schachte stated with humor. "I bought a motorcycle. I think back on that time now when Carmen and I would ride around on my motorcycle. It was a Honda 160 'SuperSport.' On Sundays when we would go to Mass the girls in those days wore crinolines, and so she would get on the motorcycle behind me riding side-saddle so that her dress would not fly up in the air. She would hold it down. We used that little motorcycle for everything. They became a popular mode of transportation on Navy bases.

"I remember riding to the beach one day—just the two of us—no helmets, no nothing. I was in short sleeves and short pants. In a material sense, we didn't have much at all, but we had each other and a zest for life," Schachte reflected. "We were spontaneous. We took our time to enjoy what little we had and to go on short excursions for the experience. They remain rich memories for us."

"Those were carefree days when we had just gotten married and spent every available moment together," Schachte reminisced. "Carmen depended on me, and I depended on her. It was a beautiful relationship from the outset."

Those days would end abruptly by a patriotic decision.

"It was later, when I brought up my sincere willingness to serve the country where they needed me most, that the conversation became deeply serious. I volunteered for combat duty in Vietnam on the small boats. This was a very difficult conversation to have with a young bride who had never lived anywhere else."

The course of their marriage would stretch outside each of their comfort zones. Additionally, Carmen had become pregnant. Their first child, Billy, was born in Puerto Rico. They had been married only two years.

"I wanted to serve in a more meaningful way. I told Carmen that I thought my orders would take a while to go through the process. It turned out that I received message orders. Message orders are much like receiving a telegram. After my commander put an endorsement on my letter requesting that duty, I knew that I would be assigned in a very short time."

"I thought, 'Oh, my Lord! I have to explain the message orders to Carmen. By this time, Billy was not even a year old. He was just a little fellow. Honestly, I felt like a fraud walking around downtown in Norfolk or San Juan, and there was a war going on. In spite of the media portrayal and the demonstrations, I knew it was the right course for me. None of that public protesting bothered me. I was in the Navy uniform, and I felt I had a Navy duty to perform."

Schachte's desire to serve the country had deep roots and grew out of his father's mentorship and his ongoing service to the Charleston Naval

Shipyard. The Charleston Shipyard was vital to the interests of the United States Navy.

"The circumstances were that I had volunteered and had gotten the message orders. Before I knew it, I was in Swift Boat training in the Coronado, California. Most serving had little money to bring dependents along to temporary duty stations. But we had saved up enough so that Carmen and Billy could join me. Carmen had one suitcase then--I will always remember. She packed it full of plastic plates and cups because we had to set up home in a motel.

"Some years later, as an admiral, we were back in that same area, and we went to that motel to check it out. It was a 'Back to the Future' experience. The motel was there—but instead of the big beautiful swimming pool where I have an old photo of Carmen and Billy in the water, it had been filled in. There was a palm tree growing out of the middle where the pool area once was. I also found our old rental place at Imperial Beach. It had been owned by a very nice lady whose son was flying off a carrier near the coast of Vietnam. She was so very kind to us. That old rental house was still there. It brought back great memories for us," Schachte reflected. "Those were the places that launched my combat training and Vietnam experience."

The young Navy couple roughed it during the training period. Carmen would become a single parent with an infant for the difficult year of 1968.

"That was a tough time going through that training, but the thought that I would soon be leaving my loving little family to go half-way around the world was the most difficult part. In fact, the night before I left to go to Vietnam as a volunteer was the second most difficult night of my life. The first being when I found out that my Dad had died suddenly of a massive heart attack just after turning 59," Schachte detailed.

Leaving for Vietnam came too fast for the young Schachtes.

"Initially, we made the best of it in this old motel. Carmen and I spent our 1967 Christmas together in Southern California. We enjoyed New Year's Eve at the Officer's Club there. On New Year's Day, when we were both melancholic because I was leaving for Vietnam the next day, we went to the Pasadena area to see the parade. Never having been in the Rose Bowl traffic before, it took quite a while to get back to our place on Imperial Beach," Schachte retold. "It was good to occupy that time with something fun and memorable."

The next day, January 2, was a very emotional parting.

Schachte described the touching experience. "With so much departure concern for Carmen and little Billy, I left for the duty I felt obliged to perform. I was saddened, as was Carmen. You just don't know if it's the last time that you will see your loved ones. It was a very difficult goodbye, but amid tears Carmen remained positive and optimistic. She was my every reason and hope to survive this demanding combat tour."

The year 1968 went by all too slowly.

After Schachte flew out through "SeaTac" (Seattle-Tacoma Airport) to Vietnam, Carmen returned to Charleston with little Billy. She stayed with the Schachte family on Grove Street for a week before going back to stay with her parents in Puerto Rico. There, for the remainder of the year, Carmen and young Billy awaited a positive outcome despite the evening news reports after the TET Offensive began. Carmen saw the reports on nightly news programs that her husband could not imagine. The public sentiment shift became vigilant.

"I knew that the man I loved was doing his duty the only way he knew," Carmen recalled. "Yet the protests were growing, and the war was becoming so unpopular at home that returning soldiers were not wearing their uniforms. They were being punished for their service to the country. It was difficult for all of the military families."

"And so many were burning draft cards and moving to Canada. I prayed for one simple gift—the safe return of my husband," Carmen stated. "He meant everything to me."

Late December 1968 could not arrive fast enough. Schachte received his orders to return. His intermediate stop during his leave between duty stations would be to Charleston on his way to Rochester, New York. Carmen immediately left for Charleston with little Billy in tow. She would arrive in time to spend a happy reunion with her husband at his Grove Street home. It was a joy-filled time, despite the uncertainty that surrounded the late 1960s.

Carmen and Billy Schachte, 2019. Schachte family Archive.

The new assignment in upstate New York was a new beginning for the young Schachtes. The service commitment in Rochester was shortened by the good fortune of Lieutenant Schachte's being accepted into law school. The Schachtes moved to Columbia, South Carolina, for a three-year course of study in the law in the summer of 1969.

"Arriving in Columbia, we decided to buy our first home. We lived our early marriage frugally, to the point that when we got ready to buy where I started law school, we had no credit rating because we had no credit cards. I contacted a gentleman banker in Charleston who wrote a letter of recommendation on my behalf.

"The gentleman banker lent me tuition money back while I was at Clemson—and I diligently paid it back. Not many people had money in Charleston back then. In fact, I had to drop out of Clemson for a semester to work. I worked for Ruscon Construction Company for a dollar an hour and saved enough—and with a small loan—I resumed my studies. When I graduated, I promptly paid off that emergency student loan."

The promptness of Schachte's loan repayment and the financial relationship he had forged became consequential when it was time to buy a home.

"We were able to get a mortgage for the house. I also decided to get a credit card—having had none, not even a credit card for gas.

The first time I used that credit card was to buy flowers for Carmen to bring to the hospital after she delivered our second son, David," Schachte remembered.

His frugality was not unlike most of the Charleston community. The city had been through excruciating economic times—more so than most of the country. The financial repercussions lingered from the devastating Civil War, the constant hurricanes, and the Great Earthquake of 1886. Charleston's economic malaise lasted a full century.

Schachte coyly described his financial philosophy.

"I really believed in 'high finance.' If the cost was too *high* and you had to *finance*, you didn't need it."

The first use of the credit card for Carmen's flowers upon David's birth had a fitting tribute later in the admiral's career.

"It was much later in life when I had recently been selected for rear admiral, lower half. There was a promotion ceremony in the Secretary of the Navy's private dining room in the Pentagon. I had gotten a dozen roses wrapped in a box with a nice bow to surprise Carmen. After I was promoted, and that part of the ceremony was over, I took a moment to hand Carmen the flowers," he retold the story.

"She opened the box and exclaimed to everyone in the room, 'Gosh, look at the flowers, and I didn't even have a baby!' All laughed but me because it was very true and very meaningful in my life," Schachte grinned. "I then went on to thank her for her constant support and love and, 'the occasional heavy dose of constructive criticism.'"

Admiral and Mrs. Billy Schachte as Parade Marshal St. Patrick's Day 2018. Photo courtesy Schachte Family archives.

A merger of commitment and complement compelled the Schachtes.

"It has always been a partnership marriage. Carmen provided much to me where I was deficient. And I wanted to be there for her always for the things she needed of me. We completed each other throughout a happy lifetime in that way."

The mutual devotion remains, and it shines brightly.

CHAPTER 6
Swift Boats on the South China Sea

"Try to stay calm with every situation, and you'll handle it with intelligence, respect, and the willingness to act. Duty superseded self. It was the formula we all knew that gave us the best opportunity for success and to live another day," Schachte recalled of the harrowing times.

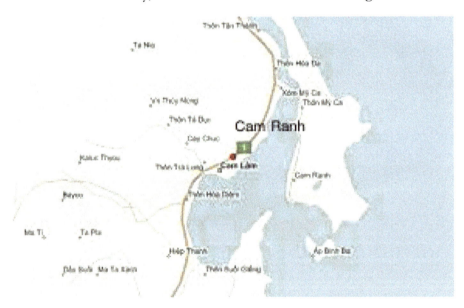

Cam Ranh Bay became the focus of Viet Cong resupply traffic in 1968.[38]

"I departed the States for Vietnam on January 2, 1968. I arrived in Vietnam about three weeks before the TET offensive began. Interestingly, I saw an article in the New York Times in the Opinion section recently. I saved it. The name of the article was 'The Skunk Alpha Encounter.' This article appeared on July 14, 2017.[39] A "skunk" is a suspected enemy ship in disguise. The alpha designation refers to the first suspected enemy ship of that particular day's patrol."[40] Schachte explained.

"The Skunk Alpha encounter involved a Swift Boat sea battle with a 200-feet long pseudo-trawler. The unflagged 'Skunk Alpha' trawler was loaded with resupply weaponry for the Viet Cong." Schachte recalled the incident.

"According to the after-action report cited in the *New York Times* article, 'The trawler was loaded with more than 90 tons of weapons and ammunition, including recoilless rifles, rockets and rocket launchers, TNT, electric detonators and cord, heavy machine guns, grenades and more than 1,000 automatic rifles.'[41] Patrolling the Vietnam Coast was dangerous duty. These trawlers, when detected and confronted, were likely to respond with much hidden firepower." He stated.

Schachte further explained by recalling his own Skunk Alpha encounter.

"The Skunk Alpha article reminded me of a similar encounter I had while in Vietnam. It was engaging a trawler which was one of three trawlers that were involved in a TET resupply mission out of Hanain Island in China. Our reconnaissance people had picked these trawlers up as they were headed south and tracked them. The one I was involved in was headed for Mavic Mountain—which had a bay surrounding it with a natural port. I think the water dropped to forty feet right at the shoreline. As it turned out, all the boats in my division scrambled to intercept," he stated. "We patrolled the coast for these enemy activities."

*A typical trawler used by the Viet Cong for resupply
Photo from New York Times article "Skunk Alpha."*

"Our on-scene tactical and Division Commander, then-Lieutenant Commander Skip Hibbard, was highly respected and a courageous person. He had a great sense of humor—a good guy. In a difficult situation there was such collegiality all around. We always had Skip Hibbard ensuring the chain of command was followed and military matters such as that were observed. That night, Sector Headquarters directed that all boats were to scramble out to intercept the trawler which was in one of our operating areas north of Nha Trang," Schachte recalled.

Nha Trang is a large coastal Vietnamese city.

"I was off-duty ashore with my crew. We had come in the day before after operating over thirty hours, and we had the night off. I was in my quarters when one of the enlisted men from our radio section came in and said for me to take a call from Sector headquarters. I was informed that we were to scramble the only boat left in our port, the '68 boat' which had just returned from overhaul in Yokosuka, Japan. The boat was not fully operational, and it was not until I got on board with my crew that I learned the extent of it—radar was down and not working, the Fox Mike radio was not working, the side band radio was up, we were short of flak jackets, there was only one 50-caliber machine gun forward and we had to secure that with a piece of manila line. After securing the bolt rig and the rear mount 50-caliber, and seeing that the 81-millimeter mortar piggyback was in good shape and mounted, we had to move quickly. We had no 'H.E.' (high explosive) ammo or any kind of mortar ammunition."

Schachte described the stark realities of a not-ready-for-action vessel.

There were few times for leisure while patrolling the coast of Vietnam. (Schachte family archives.)

"We loaded the only mortar rounds available—several cases of white phosphorus, or as we called it, 'Willy Peter,' exposed on the fantail. I was directed to pick up an interpreter at the small Vietnamese navy base directly across from our piers. I stopped by and picked up a young sailor. Off we went. We were traveling at flank speed island hopping, fortunately on a moonlit night," Schachte continued.

Flank speed is the term used to describe a naval vessel's speed that is higher than the maximum rating for the vessel.[42]

"When we got past Nha Trang and entered into the bay at Mavic Mountain, we immediately saw a heavy-duty firefight ongoing. Skip Hibbard had his boats deployed in a manner that provided him maximum fire power onto the trawler."

The admiral's recollection of the incident was dramatic.

"I radioed Sector that we were going to close the firefight on my sideband radio, and, as we proceeded to join the firefight, the trawler suddenly exploded. It blew debris sky-high. In fact, there was a 'Puff the Magic Dragon aircraft' coming in to provide machine gun support, and I was on sideband radio—as was the pilot of that aircraft. He had been alerted that I had no Fox Mike and the best way to contact would be on sideband radio."

The close air support Douglas AC 47 was nicknamed "Puff the Magic Dragon."[43] It was developed for the Vietnam War. The gunship was deployed by the United States Air Force. It became useful because of its lethal close-support fire power.[44]

"It was dangerously humorous. The pilot got on the radio and announced, 'You sailors almost got us with that one. We had crap flying around us after that explosion. By the way, you sailors also broke up one hell of a poker game for us to get out here and join you.' You can bet I was glad that pilot was there to help in the middle of that fire fight," Schachte recalled.

Part of the mission was to establish the identity of fishermen and search for contraband weapons. Schachte (L) commanded a Swift Boat for that purpose. Photo courtesy of Schachte family archives.

"So, I was directed to close the beach and begin psychological operations or 'PSYOPS' with our interpreter which we did patrolling back and forth off the coast with the typical Vietnamese language call to 'stop and surrender,' and that sort of thing. I then got a flash on the sideband radio from sector to clear the area 'bombing aircraft in route.' I was sitting at the controls and immediately turned the boat around and headed out to sea, again at flank speed, outrunning the bombs that were being dropped by a B-52. The bombing caused large waves to occur in the ocean and in the bay area. It didn't provide any problems for us, but those Swift boats are not really that stable in that kind of environment."

Swift boats were made in New Orleans and had light aluminum hulls.[45] The idea came from transport vessels used to transit workers to and from the Gulf of New Mexico oil rigs. The boats were fifty feet long with a shallow five-foot draft. They were considered effective patrol deterrents near the Vietnam coastline but had a tendency to roll in rough waters because they were considered too light for the open ocean. The aluminum also left little protection for the sailors under enemy attack.[46]

"I later learned that this B-52 had been on a bombing raid elsewhere, and some of its load was left and was therefore diverted to the Op area where we were with the sunken trawler. The next morning at first light some South Koreans appeared on the shoreline, and I was also able to see some of the destruction from the night before. One thing I will always remember was a Viet Cong body that was laying on a large rock boulder at the entrance to the cove. The South Koreans saw that and went up and poured gasoline on that body and torched it. They later told me that was for sanitary reasons.

"The South Koreans that were on the beach immediately started undressing, and I realized quickly that they were putting on scuba gear and they hit the water. About this time a Vietnamese navy boat radioed me—the American advisor onboard did—he came along side and asked that I be very careful because the Vietnamese were afraid the South Koreans were going to go aboard the sunken trawler. After it sunk, there were cases of AK47 packed in cosmoline floating on the surface along with huge containers of East German medical supplies and those kinds of things. So, I put my boat between the shoreline and the Vietnamese and the South Koreans without incident. But I had to maintain that position most of that day, and we weren't relieved until the next afternoon," Schachte described the mission.

"By the time I got back to home port, I learned the details of Commander Hibbard's heroic actions in directing the fight against the enemy trawler and the fact that there were two other trawlers likewise that were sunk in different areas along the coast. I might add, that my crew had rightfully been in the enlisted club when we were notified to scramble the 68 Boat—our Swift Boat—and after we were underway about ten minutes or so, I quickly realized that our Vietnamese interpreter and I were the only ones completely sober on our boat. But everything turned out well in the end."

There were other hazards that were not related to the conflict.

"When SWIFT Boats originally started boarding and searching junks to check the IDs of occupants and search for contraband, we would pull up alongside a junk and tie it up using lines they provided. The VC became aware of this standard method of operation (MO). Once, one of the junk occupants pretended to get a line to throw up to the attending SWIFT Boat but instead was pulling the pin on a hand grenade. The occupant tossed it into the machine gun mount on top of the pilot house killing the Navy gunner.

"The MO was changed so that the SWIFT Boat would throw a line to the junk to be boarded. Invariably, these operations occurred around 3:00 A.M. After boarding and inspecting a junk, someone would forget to get all of those lines back on board. The line in the water often wrapped around one of the SWIFT Boat's powerful twin propellers. When this happened, one of the boat crew had to jump in the water wearing a mask and carrying a knife. We directed lighting from the boats. The lights could attract the extremely poisonous South China sea snakes. The crew member who went in the water also had a rope tied around his waist so he could be alerted if sea snakes were detected. When this happened on my boat, I would position myself on the stern with a double-aught buck sawed-off pump shot gun to ward away the snakes while our swimmer was still in the water. That MO worked, and we never suffered of a fatality from sea snake bites.

The admiral continued the point. "I had to use that shot gun more than once depending how close to the shore we were—which was then almost every time we had a person in the water. That was not a sound that the swimmer wanted to hear!"

"The point is that SWIFT Boat training did not include many of these unplanned but frequent hazards. And the boats themselves, by their shallow aluminum hulls meant engineered instability in the open waters," Schachte summarized. "We kept ours above the water line for the duration. For that, I am thankful."

The days and nights were harrowing during and after the TET offensive. Every day and every duty brought with it the specter of confrontation, conflict, and calamity. There were no easy days. There was no moment of relaxation for the sailors, soldiers, Marines, and airmen who were there to perform a duty—one that was becoming more unpopular with every nightly news report.

The Vietnam War did not end until 1975.[47] Schachte reflected upon his service in the controversial conflict.

"Upon returning from Vietnam, I had often been asked about being scared. While I generally never talked about things like that, the answer has always been, 'Of course I have been scared—been scared an awful lot while in Vietnam.' There were several highlights of fright. The first in my memory was the time as I closed to join that firefight mentioned earlier, and, as I did, the trawler exploded. Commander Hibbard and his team and I had joined that firefight. It was unnerving going around the bend and heading into the Bay and seeing tracers of fire going both ways. The enemy trawler was using an anti-aircraft machine gun, a 14.5-millimeter gun. Our Swift Boats were using our 50-caliber guns.

"Another time, I was standing off the coast in an area not too far from the Bay of Mavic Mountain while there was a firefight ongoing between a company of South Korean forces and the Viet Cong and NVA (North Vietnamese Army). A South Korean colonel was seriously wounded in the firefight, and I was asked to stay in the vicinity. I was trawling back and forth parallel to the shoreline, and they were going to send a South Korean colonel out to me in a Vietnamese Junk. I was to pick him up and take him to high seas for pickup by a Dustoff Medevac[48] helicopter.

A "Dustoff Medevac" was an unarmed medical emergency craft, whether helicopter or other transport. They were well-marked and protected by the Geneva Convention.[49]

"That was the plan anyway. We were driving back and forth looking at the firefight that was taking place along the shoreline. Suddenly, my boat went up in the air coming from the right bow and my machine gunner in the tub above the pilot house got soaking wet. The water explosion nearly immersed the boat. It didn't turn over, but it was very unstable. I was sitting at the controls, and I picked up the radio and called my counterpart who was with the South Koreans on the beach and reminded him that it was us in that vicinity. We had just received what looked like recoilless rifle fire.

"He answered back immediately, 'Only small arms at this location.' As I was sitting at the controls of the boat, I hit flank speed, and off we went for open seas. As we took off, rounds started landing in our wake behind us. The enemy fire actually walked right up behind us as we headed for high seas. I was told to stand off again, but the rescue plan was different. That South Korean colonel was not expected to survive. That was a very scary moment."

"Interestingly, a couple months later, another of our Swift Boats was in that same general area and took fire from a recoilless rifle (similar to a tube rocket launcher), and our boat returned fire with mortars. We had a reconnaissance done the next day and they found the weapon and three dead VC in the vicinity of the weapon. The boat officer who conducted that accurate firing was a fellow from North Carolina—a lieutenant junior grade. I might add that he played tackle for the University of North Carolina football team, which was not unusual. All Swift Boat skippers were volunteers. For some reason on the Swift Boats we had a lot of jocks, former football players—guys who knew challenges."

Schachte knew well the sudden rush of adrenaline and the benefit of fear as it pertained to battle sequences. He knew that the reaction would need to be structured and centered upon the duty expected.

"You do what is necessary. Other than the routine fear that comes about anytime we open fire, there was another time that really stands out in my mind," Schachte considered.

"I was in port while our division commander, Skip Hibbard, was out with a patrol group, and, as the executive officer, I was the 'senior officer on the beach,' as we say in the Navy. I was in my room and one of the enlisted men from our radio shack came to me and said you have to get down to the pier, Mr. Schachte. There is something going on down there with one of the members of a crew. I immediately hopped into the jeep and drove down to the pier, and I got there and found out one of the members of a crew had apparently flipped out, and they didn't know what condition he was in other than he was sitting alone at the end of the pier—sitting on a bollard.

"I found out that we had a sniper set up on one of the adjacent piers. And I directed that they not do anything unless something serious happened. So, I walked down the pier by myself and when I got almost to the end of the pier where this fellow was sitting, he stood up and pulled a 38-caliber pistol from where he was sitting. It could not be seen until I got close to him. He cocked it and put it right close to my forehead. It was almost humorous because the guys monitoring everything said I was walking out and without skipping a beat I started walking backwards. Thank God he didn't shoot. He lowered the weapon, and we knew we had a breakdown situation," Schachte retold. "It was a tense confrontation."

Other actions were ordered.

"We contacted this young man's boat officer immediately. He came out and talked to him, and we found out that he was just very confused and upset about a lot of things. That was one of the dangers of Vietnam—with all the weapons everywhere—if somebody ever flipped out, they could cause a lot of damage. His boat officer got him to turn over his pistol to him. He, this young man, and I were walking off the pier—about midway off the pier, when this young man looked at me and said, 'Mr. Schachte here…take this.'

"He reached in his back area and pulled out a K-bar—a big knife. I could see how sharp it was, it was glittering in the middle of the full moon night. We had an Air Force hospital ambulance standing by with a straightjacket, and so we got that young man to them, and they took off with him. He was eventually Medevac'd to the States." Schachte recalled the resolution. "Battle fatigue, nervous stress, mental illness, traumatic symptoms—you name it. They were all possible in the crucible of conflict."

The dangers in Vietnam proved to be broader than the enemy combatants.

"Having so many weapons around was always a potential problem. And then there were mistakes made that resulted in casualties."

Schachte explained by a story he knew.

"There was a base north of Nha Trang at Vung Ro Bay which was run by an Army lieutenant colonel. There was always a lot of drinking going on in that small little army base, and he got so concerned about weapons being so readily available, he had all the M-16s locked up at night. About three days later they were hit by an enemy sapper squad (military engineering squad), and two of his men were killed trying to get to their own weapons. The weapons had been locked down."

Schachte continued.

"Tragically, we lost a young Navy lieutenant junior grade that night. The young fellow was a Naval Academy graduate who had been in the country only a week when the firefight started. His roommate who had been there for a while dove underneath his bed...there in a little hooch (military slang for hut). The young fellow who was new to the country went outside to see what was happening and was killed instantly—shot in the head. There were no lights on in the room and it was a moonless night. The VC sprayed more fire into the hooch and missed his roommate. It was sad to lose anyone, especially that young man who had just reported for duty. He was assigned to work in that base right on the waterfront. The Army disciplined the individual who had the weapons locked up. I don't know what happened to him, but he was relieved by two bird colonels, as I recall."

The TET Offensive became the signature event of 1968 in Vietnam—the full year of Schachte's service in country. The concerted effort was launched by the Viet Cong and the North Vietnamese to push the battle lines southward and control the war. That period between the end of January and end of May resulted in the loss of 7,040 American lives.[50]

Schachte recalled the events. They left lasting memories and many nightmares.

He missed a pivotal year in American history back home. 1968 would become a turning point of social and political upheaval in the United States. Martin Luther King was assassinated in Memphis. The great orator and peacemaker came to Memphis to support a strike of sanitation workers.[51] Race riots broke out, and fires destroyed cars and homes in Baltimore, Chicago, Kansas City, and Washington, DC.[52] Peace marches dominated the evening news. There were marches on Washington, and controversial protests—even at the Summer Olympics in Mexico City. Other protests were significant—like the Cesar Chavez hunger strike to raise awareness of the low wages of itinerant workers in California's vegetable, fruit, and wine industries.[53] The young white generation protested, too. Their sentiments extended beyond the controversial Vietnam War. There remained a generational rejection of previous societal mores and traditions, from haircuts to sex to drugs. The peace sign became prominent.

The signs of the times in 1968. Photos from general sources.

In the political world, the country was shocked again by gruesome violence. Bobby Kennedy, the Democratic frontrunner for the nomination to run against eventual Republican candidate Richard Nixon was shot and killed in Los Angeles on June 5.[54] Hubert Humphrey became the nominee. But the summertime Democratic National Convention in Chicago was mired in constant protests. Newsreels full of police tear gas and scrambling young protestors dominated the news.[55] Richard Nixon won the November 1968 presidential election.[56]

Schachte's 1968 tour of duty in Vietnam missed these caustic upheavals and the nightly news reports that brought the intensity of war into American homes.

Ironically, 1968 ended on a calm and spiritual note as the Apollo 8 astronauts slung around the dark side of the moon on December 31, 1968 and recited from the Book of Genesis as Planet Earth rose in their view.[57] It was a good transition for Billy Schachte's arrival home. He landed at the Charleston Airport that day—Christmas Eve of 1968.

"For a solid year we were intensely focused upon the duty at hand, the responsibilities of protecting those under my command, and the sheer savagery of spontaneous enemy action. It was a massive weight to bear. Any soldier or sailor will tell you that duty in a war zone remains intense twenty-four-seven. There were few breaks," Schachte reflected. "You plan and you prepare—and even then, you can be unlucky. The frayed nerves and the sight of death gave rise to the condition we now call PTS, or Post-Traumatic Stress. It's real."

The 58,220 American deaths in Vietnam included 7,878 military officers.[58] The winnable war remains a controversy by way of its treatment of returning veterans, the horrid loss of American lives, and the ultimate withdrawal from what was politically considered an endless morass. No one came back unaffected.

CHAPTER 7

In the Crosshairs

There is another incident that re-emerges in the admiral's memory.

"After the Tet Offensive, I was assigned to be the executive officer and operations officer –XO/OP—after the prior incumbent's year in Vietnam was up and he returned to the States." Schachte stated.

The Tet Offensive was named for the first day of the lunar new year in Vietnam.[59]

"In my new position I was also our Division's Intelligence Officer. As XO my duties consisted of, among other things, holding a daily 3:00 p.m. briefing during which I passed along pertinent intelligence and presided over each boat officers debrief of their previously assigned operation area along the 120 miles of coastal areas and rivers that were our responsibility," Schachte revealed.

"We held these daily briefings in a fairly large room in our Division Headquarters which contained a huge chart detailing our area of responsibility. The daily briefings were held seven days a week. After I first arrived at our division, I noticed that a popular watch among the officers was a Seiko that not only featured the date and time but also the day of the week. That was a significant feature because, in Vietnam, a soldier or sailor would often lose track of what day of the week it was. Those watches became popular.

"Right after Tet, in-country intel (Intelligence Operations) began forecasting potential flare ups. Post-Tet was a different story where we were, and we began getting enemy debriefs—information that someone would glean from captured enemy or other pertinent sources. Some of the intel was worthy of note during our daily debriefs."

Schachte continued.

"One shocking incident was the debrief of the successful interrogation of a former VC sniper. He revealed that he had been assigned to take out a Swift Boat skipper. I realized that we were actually easy to detect wearing khaki pants (as the crew wore Navy blue jeans). Officers normally donned a flak jacket over a light green tee shirt if in an active area. That VC intel report advised that on a certain date in area 4H (our southern-most operations area in a bay around Phan Rang city) there was this enemy sniper positioned in an attempt to take out an American Navy officer. The sniper was set up and actually had the targeted officer in his sights—ready to execute—when a village chief from that area intervened and pleaded with the sniper not to shoot. He reasoned that because "the Americans would respond forcefully and that would be very destructive to all in his village." Based on the emotional chief's urging the sniper agreed to take his business elsewhere. We ascertained later that the sniper got those in charge to change assignments away from our Swift Boats. The report had an immediate and concerning effect to me personally.

"As I further read the extensive ROI (results of interview), the sniper mentioned the time and date of the incident and went on to say that his targeted officer was sitting on a Swift Boat forward air vent eating an apple and smoking a cigarette. That struck a note with me because during a slack time on patrol I had done that. The apple and the cigarette rang a bell with me. I immediately checked further in our office patrol assignment logs and discovered my Swift Boat was in that operations area on that day—and therefore—that was me in his cross hairs when the village chief intervened. I immediately had that familiar gut twang. It was a sick feeling. I could have been sent back in a flag-draped box," Schachte confided.

"Since it was over and the sniper was in custody, I elected not to pass the detailed information on. It was nothing to brag about. We all knew there were unknown dangers to be faced when we went out on patrol. Dying by sniper fire could be a given." Schachte concluded.

*Lt. Schachte peers the shore of Vietnam 1968.
Photo courtesy of Schachte family archives.*

"After our tremendous successes during Tet, our division's activities then dropped dramatically. In fact, I was astonished about that time to get a letter from my dad expressing concern over what was being reported on the national news about all the Tet-related combat that was continuing. That was certainly not the case in our operations area. In fact, it was about this time that our leaders began plans for major Swift Boat operations in the southern delta area of Vietnam. Then came the bombing halt. Much had changed. Those things changed in Washington—not in our small and potentially terrifying corner of Southeast Asia," Schachte presumed.

He would know more about those boardroom decisions years later.

The duty of a sailor or a soldier in wartime in a war zone is, by definition, fraught with danger. Schachte summarized his Vietnam activity of 1968.

"I participated in more than ninety combat patrols, naval gunfire support missions, civic action programs, and special operations against the enemy," he stated in a reflection.

His actions as a young Navy Lieutenant merited the Bronze Star with a 'V.' He was the epitome of a professional naval officer serving in the most trying of circumstances—armed conflict against an elusive enemy combatant. The Vietnam experience was real with daily reminders on newscasts and troop reports. The Killed-in-Action (KIAs) and Missing in Action (MIAs) lists were daunting. Schachte did not want to raise either number.

One can never assimilate war. The training for combat and the reality of combat cannot be equated. In training, there is a start time and an end time coordinated. In the Vietnam War, both were excruciatingly undefined.

"The war was becoming quite unpopular at home, but the soldiers and sailors there were not a part of the decisions. They were in the fray. And they were acquitting themselves well. The record shows that," Schachte reflected. "It was the media that divided the justifications, the enthusiasm, and the politics. We were there as sworn members of the greatest military the world had known, and the men I served with carried out our assigned duties honorably."

But the attitude on college campuses had changed. Some of the vitriol was warranted, but so much more was misdirected to the returning veterans.

"And, as we later learned, intelligence records revealed that the Soviet Union invested impressive amounts of currency in a stealth campaign to move the American people against the war. I read years later from intelligence sources that there was more Russian money spent to dissuade the American war effort than was given to Cuba," Schachte cited.

These revelations came well after the Vietnam War, via the media and counter-intelligence sources.[60]

CHAPTER 8
The Return of the Sailor

The old Charleston SC Municipal Airport. Passengers were loaded and unloaded outside regardless of weather.

With his full-year tour of duty winding down, there was a chance that he could return to Carmen and the family by Christmas Day. He would do all that he could to be there for a joyful reunion.

"My best Christmas ever occurred in 1968. That was the Christmas morning when I returned from Vietnam. My flight had been delayed 18 hours out of Vietnam, so all of my connections were fouled up. I remember catching a red-eye from Chicago to Atlanta and then an early flight from Atlanta to Charleston. We were told to change to civvies when we got to America because of the protesters. In my carry-on bag I brought a pair of civilian pants and a sports shirt. I guess I was too proud of my compatriots who had sacrificed—and some who had died. I refused to wear the civilian clothes. I was proud to be a member of my country's military forces. I would deal with whatever epithets were slung at me in reverence to those I really cared about—the others who experienced the hardness of war in a foreign country."

The admiral continued to detail the memory of his exuberant return to Charleston.

"I knew that some of my friends had some ugly experiences on their way back from Vietnam. I knew these things, but I was not going to shy away from wearing my country's uniform for any reason," Schachte announced proudly. "I swore an allegiance to my country. That uniform was part of that allegiance."

But getting home was very difficult.

"When my ticket was confirmed, I called home to tell Carmen and my dad what my travel plan was. It was just so reassuring to hear their voices again. When my mother got on the phone after Carmen, I hadn't heard her voice in over a year.

"The emotions rushed in. I was almost embarrassed. I was standing there with some Marine enlisted guys in line to use the pay phone in the airport in Atlanta. I was so overcome, and I almost lost it hearing the voices of those I loved and missed so much," he recalled. "Those Marines saw this Navy lieutenant really get caught up in the moment."

The flight was less than an hour to the old dilapidated Charleston airport. Schachte got in on Christmas Eve.

"When I got off that plane in Charleston, it was marvelous to see them standing there. Carmen was there, and my oldest son, Billy. They had been in Puerto Rico the year I was gone. Young Billy only spoke Spanish. Mom and Dad were there, too. They all came to get me. I remember thinking, 'God, I made it home alive. I am home with my loved ones at last.' So, that was clearly my most memorable Christmas ever," he beamed.

"I also remember going to 9:00 a.m. Mass on that Christmas morning. It was great to be back in the church of my youth, Sacred Heart, and to thank God again for delivering me back to my family."

There was an immediate odyssey to the return. Some of his dear friends were unaware of his plight.

"My dear friend Freddy McMahon, whom I hadn't seen in quite a while, saw me after church. He smiled. He asked me how I got such a suntan—and I was pretty tanned. I realized he might not have known that I had spent the previous year in Vietnam. I said sheepishly, 'Freddy, I just got home from Vietnam.' I thought that would merit his surprise or that he would ask a military question—or be happy that I made it back."

But Schachte received a much-different response.

"He said, 'Yes, but they have monsoons there. I assumed that Vietnam didn't have that much sunshine.'

"I replied, 'What can I say?' I didn't want to challenge his image of what he saw on TV where they showed nightly films of depressed areas, as if the whole country were made of mud. There are extraordinarily hot days in Southeast Asia. You cannot avoid the intense sun there," Schachte intimated. "Besides that, if you hadn't been, you probably couldn't possibly describe it properly—even to your best childhood friends."

It was time to embark upon a new direction, but the options were limited.

"My next assignment was Rochester, New York. I would be assigned to the ROTC unit there. It was pretty much during the heyday of the SDS (Students for a Democratic Society) and they had a very strong chapter on the campus of Rochester University. It was a time of protests in America, and ROTC units were the main target," Schachte reminded. "The times were counter to the military sense of duty."

He would report to the ROTC unit. His contractual commitment to the Navy was still in place.

"I was still not sure I would make it a career. My time in Rochester would define that issue. In going there, I knew I wanted to try to get into law school, but those chances were remote. But I was young, happily married, a father, and had my whole life ahead after Vietnam. I was optimistic that things would get better for me—either in the Navy or in private life back in Charleston."

Naval ships in port. The Navy is ever at the ready to defend U.S. interests and freedoms. Photo courtesy U.S. Navy

CHAPTER 9

Directed Sadness, Rochester

"When I reported to Rochester with the ROTC detachment, I also was charged with a somber duty no officer wants. Within weeks, I became the CACO (Casualty Assistance Calls Officer) at that unit. The casualty assistance is usually a duty performed by Military Chaplains. Our CO called me in to advise that he was assigning me additional duty as CACO Officer for Monroe County, New York. As part of the assignment, I would be receiving an instruction manual from the Bureau of Naval Personnel. That manual was sent to my home address. As part of my new designation, I had an around-the-clock duty with my home phone number provided. This was a duty of intense morbidity. If a serviceman or woman from Monroe County, New York, died, I was to be informed immediately. I would then personally deliver the news to the family of the deceased," Schachte explained. "You couldn't imagine how difficult this was for me after what I had experienced and seen in the past year."

The young officer was late of the Vietnam conflict, but the difficult duties lingered. He hoped that he would never be called to perform under the CACO program.

"This duty had previously been handled by a Navy chaplain assigned to a local USMC Reserve unit. But the chaplain had relocated. Several days later, the instruction booklet arrived. It contained several Washington D.C. telephone numbers for after-hours contacts. It is the protocol that the Navy or Marine Corps informed a designated next-of-kin that someone had been killed in action (KIA), or missing in action (MIA) or was seriously ill—usually wounded.

"In the instructions, I was to meet the body at the airport and conduct the military aspects of the funeral and present the flag to the designated next-of-kin. I had never heard of this program before and was not eager to get my first assigned case," Schachte intimated. "It was just one county in one state. I had hoped that Monroe County, New York, would remain unaffected when these morbid designations were doled out."

Schachte was not to remain on the sideline of CACO for long.

"Several weeks later, I received a Saturday morning call from Washington. A bow ramp in Danang had been blown up, and the person I was to represent could not be found. He was listed as a MIA. Sadly, I wrote down his parents' address, put on my uniform, and drove to our unit. There, I picked up our U.S. Navy station wagon and, since I was Catholic and the MIA was thought to be Catholic, I went to the Catholic Church nearest to the man's residence. Fortunately, the priest had been there for quite a while and knew the family. He acknowledged that he knew them but that they worshipped at another church nearby. So, I went to that church, and that pastor was there working on the next Sunday's sermon. When I told him the purpose of my visit, he called for his assistant pastor and asked him to accompany me. The assistant was a slightly older fellow and very friendly. When I got to the designated address, we walked up on the front porch. I knew that I was entirely out of my element. These were destined to be emotional events that one can never forget. I rang the doorbell.

"The front door had three paneled windows. I was standing to the right of the minister and could see who answered. The person answering the door turned out to be the young man's mother. The first person she saw was the minister, and when she did, she smiled beautifully. But then she saw me, deduced the situation, and let out a scream. Her husband came running out of the bathroom where he had been shaving, and a half of his face was still full of lather. It was an awful experience to witness," Schachte recalled the vivid details.

"We entered the house and—to my disappointment—the minister, instead of informing the parents of the reason for our visit, turned to me and said, 'The Lieutenant has something to tell you.'" Schachte described the moment.

"I managed to get it all out without a lot of detail and then hugged his mom and dad smudging a little shaving lather in the process. After ensuring I had everyone's phone number we left, and I returned the minister to his church. I was deeply touched by it all and couldn't help but think of the aftermath to that Rochester family. I went back to the university and picked up my car and drove home to Carmen and Billy."

The dutiful lieutenant continued.

"My required tasks were still incomplete. I met the casket at the airport. The total weight of the identified remains was only sixty-five pounds. I was responsible for helping the family conduct the funeral, and I personally presented the flag to his mother on behalf of a grateful nation. The burial had to wait until the ground was no longer frozen.

"In the extended process, I had called and visited with the family numerous times. After the funeral, the young man's uncle invited his mother and father and me and Carmen out to dinner at a very nice restaurant. They were understandably devastated. Yet they took the time to thank us."

The awkwardness of the duty to inform has no specific training—just a manual and a protocol. Schachte had to be strong and helpful to these impacted Gold Star families. His abilities came from his own sturdy family foundations and his innate spiritual strength.

"My second—and fortunately my last CACO assignment (because our C.O. advised that this duty was to be shared among all Lieutenants) occurred on a Tuesday morning.

"I received the call at our unit. It was a 'ser-ill' (seriously ill or usually badly wounded), but the young man was already being evacuated and in stable condition. As I was already in uniform, I got into our designated U.S. Navy station wagon and drove to the address. When I got to the address, several kids were playing inside. A lady who identified herself as an aunt was tending to the children and advised the father was working a day shift. She informed me that he would be arriving shortly and invited me to sit in the living room. I did so. When the father came, he seemed pretty solemn and said he had seen the car and asked that I join him in the kitchen for a beer--something frowned upon in this situation. But considering I had what I thought to be—under the circumstances—good news, I joined him. As we sat around the kitchen table and I told him about his son being evacuated as wounded," Schachte remembered.

"The father still seemed quite placid. I had been trying to put as positive a spin as I could, so I asked if he were all right. His lack of outward emotion concerned me. He replied, 'Yes, I'm fine considering.'

"He thanked me for what I was doing and how personably I was performing it. But my mood really changed when he followed the comment with, 'Lieutenant, I lost my wife two weeks ago.'

"I was stunned by the revelation. The beer was his way of getting ready for the next bad circumstance, I suppose. That poor man—the father of that wounded sailor was trying to absorb the next shock of system already numbed by death. He was reeling. Likewise, I can never forget that overburdened father—ever," Schachte confided.

He thought of his own personal blessings.

"I realized that I was so lucky to have been in the line of fire, survived it, and had my dear Carmen there when I returned home. So many others—nearly 59,000 during Vietnam—had that station wagon drive up to their home and a uniformed military person they had never met get out—usually accompanied by a chaplain or a rabbi. It had to be a gut-wrenching ordeal."

Returning to the States had another consequence. Schachte wanted to advance his career and had considered trying to get into law school. But the hope of getting to law school was nearly dashed by personnel concerns at the ROTC program. Schachte would not be dismayed.

"While there in the Rochester Navy ROTC department, I had decided I really wanted to follow my dream of going to law school. I didn't keep it a secret. I applied to the University of South Carolina School of Law and was accepted after taking the LSAT. There were only four officers in that Rochester teaching unit—all were Navy lieutenants.

Rochester University, Rochester, NY. Photo courtesy of Rochester University.

"One of the fellows there had already gotten accepted into the government's Excess Leave (Law) Program, and it gave me a different idea. The program allowed the qualifier to get extended leave via the G.I. Bill, thus allowing a recipient to obtain a law degree while working through law school. I was excited when I found out about that special program, and I applied for it," Schachte recalled.

If selected, an officer would not receive pay but could find outside work to defray living costs while in law school. Upon graduation, the officer would resume a career in the Navy.

But there was a problem that Schachte had not anticipated.

"Some weeks later, I found out I had been rejected. I went to see my commanding officer at the unit then, Captain Cliff Largess. The captain told me that in his judgment, it was just an assignment officer's decision because one person was already in the program from our unit and there were only four of us there to staff the entire NROTC program. He considered the circumstance by saying, 'If another one left that would leave the program two officers short.' He further noted that the University of Rochester in New York was not a career enhancing billet for a Navy surface warfare officer," Schachte remembered.

Schachte was disappointed by the rejection, but not ultimately defeated by it.

"I talked with Carmen about it, and I had prepared my papers to resign from the Navy and then begin law school. I submitted those because I had been rejected from the law program. This became a key point in my career. At the captain's urging, I re-submitted, and the captain wrote a special fitness report on me—an officer evaluation. It was an excellent move on his part, and it salvaged my opportunity to, in fact, get into the special Excess Leave Program and go to law school. That captain's fitness report changed my career. I was ready to leave the Navy for civilian life. The report allowed me to remain in the Navy. I was on my way to law school at the University of South Carolina in Columbia."

There was another unplanned issue on the horizon.

"Before the law school acceptance, I noted that the University of Rochester did not have a law school. It had a strong liberal arts school, a medical school, and had a very high reputation in the world of academics. I started taking some courses there and came to realize that it seemed like at the end of each course, I would get very sweaty and nervous. It was unlike my previous academic experiences. And it bothered me. These incidents seemed to start after I learned that my dear friend and the person who took over my Swift Boat, Don Droz, was killed in action. In fact, one of our Navy doctors who was attending a special program in the medical school, a Navy Lieutenant in my same grade, and I became friends. I mentioned the new nervousness to him once. He said, 'Don't worry about it; that it was a hyperglycemic condition. The next time that happens, drink some orange juice with a lot of sugar in it and you will calm right down.' I took that advice," Schachte recalled.

"Well, it happened again, and I tried that formula, and nothing changed. I kept experiencing these episodes, and then when I started law school, I had some more of them. It got so bad my last year in law school, I went to see the local priest who was at the university--a very good and holy man.

I spoke to him about many things in my life. I mentioned this situation, and he told me he did not have any idea what was causing that, but that I had better monitor it. I explained to him that I had not said anything to my wife, Carmen, about these episodes."

Schachte further described the experience.

"Interestingly, later in life, I read the book *War on the Rivers* by my friend, Wey Symmes. He talked about his Vietnam combat experiences and coming home, eventually developing PTSD (currently referred to as PTS) in the form of panic attacks. It was then that I realized that what I had apparently been experiencing was just that. Those episodes eventually went away. I had never reported them to anyone. But it seems that you never know how you react to the constant duress of war. It was a normal reaction, and it subsided," Schachte resolved. "I certainly have a keen understanding of that particular condition.

"When you think about it, your body and even your mentality is that you could be attacked at any time. You cannot let your guard down. You have to be fully observant twenty-four hours a day. You may go into and out of fire zones—the actual fighting—but you are never really out of danger. It plays on your mind even when you return because you sometimes wake up thinking you are still in Vietnam," Schachte explained. "There, it was normal to wake up in a sweat."

The post-Vietnam experience had other consequences and considerations.

"While at the University in Rochester, my citation of award of the Bronze Star with 'V' arrived at our headquarters. The Captain told me he wanted to have the award presented to me in a ceremony with our Corps of Cadets on one of the days that we had a parade session. I tried to talk him out of it, saying that it would just be an opportunity for the SDS[61] to become active. He refused to listen to any of my requests. On the day of the next ROTC parade (in a gymnasium because there was so much snow on the ground) marching was impossible," Schachte retold.

SDS, or Students for a Democratic Society, was very active across the country in with a penchant to disrupt all military activities.

"The entire brigade gathered. The Captain walked to the microphone and said for me to step forward because I was going to get an award. The citation was read. But while it was being read, a large contingent of the SDS group made themselves noticeable. They started chanting, 'Baby killer, baby killer, how many babies did you kill?' In the citation, when it got down to the point of saying, 'therefor, for courage under fire and inspiring leadership' and went on, the chant got very, very loud. When I walked up to the Captain for him to pin the medal on my chest, I leaned over to him and said, 'I told you so.' He looked up at me and looked around at the rest of them and said, 'Ah, screw 'em,' and that was the way he dealt with the counterculture of the day. I did not invite Carmen to that ceremony purposely because I knew it could turn into a messy scene," Schachte retold. "The public sentiment had become aggressive and disruptive to all things military by 1969."

It was not unlike all other national and traditional military-related events. The public outcry to stop the war changed the attitude of those running for public office at every level. The media and the public demonstrations had taken their toll. Vietnam would become a difficult chapter of American history. It changed careers, and it changed people. It took decades before the Vietnam era military were accorded their just and substantial due for their honorable service and valor in a war that very few understood.

CHAPTER 10
A Tiger in Gamecock Land

The Schachtes moved yet again. But this time they were able to regroup with family members as they returned to their home state. Columbia, South Carolina, is less than two hours—110 miles—from Charleston.

"When I enrolled at law school, I was 30 years old. I was pleasantly surprised to see some of my dear friends from Clemson. Some were fraternity brothers. First and foremost were Marty Driggers and T.K. Alexander. We formed a study group. In law school, I learned it is a little different from any other course work. There are no pop quizzes. All you get is an exam at the end of the semester. So, it is a 'do or die' situation for each course. You know it, or you don't. We would get together and study and wind up arguing about the cases and what they meant. We spent hours doing that. However, for the first time, academically, I felt I was not achieving as I should. At the end of my first year, my class ranking was 239 out of 325 students."

Schachte expressed his concern that he was spending too much time arguing the cases instead of learning the critical information.

"I realized with Carmen's advice that I was not getting it done. So, I decided to drop out of that study group and started working on my own. I made 3x5 flashcards of major cases by name, and what they stood for-- and Carmen would drill me on the cases. Also, I should add that Carmen had miscarried twice when I got back from Vietnam. And we were told it would be better for her not to work. Therefore, I was a full-time student and a 40-hour per week worker. Carmen became pregnant, and our son David was born in 1972 on Carmen's birthday. It was just before my first set of exams in April of that year. Interestingly, I aced every exam I had taken after David's birth. He was born the night before my evidence exam, which was a very difficult course. I made straight A's that semester, and straight A's the semester before. I made one C and after that all the rest were A's. I graduated 30th out of 240 students. I won the award for academic achievement. My dear wife Carmen was very much a part of all of this success as she had been throughout our married life. Having David and my long study hours—and working—was a crazy time," Schachte recalled.

The University of South Carolina School of Law
Photo Courtesy University of South Carolina.

His life with Carmen became even more magical. She was the ultimate complement of a loving marriage.

"She always was a tremendous help to me at every turn. I don't ever recall being awakened at night because David was crying. She was always out of bed in a flash and into his room to take care of him. He was in a room also with his older brother, Billy. They are six years apart. At the time of Carmen's second full pregnancy, the indications were that she was going to have a girl, so we had names picked out for an expected girl. That was before the days of sonograms, or ultrasounds. The doctor was delivering what was supposed to be a 'she' until a certain point in the delivery, and he said, 'Whoops—it is not a girl.' I went home that night to meet my mother, who had driven up from Charleston to help out with Billy. Billy was so excited. Carmen and I decided that the best way to handle this since Billy had been the 'ruler of the roost' for six years, was to let Billy name his brother. In his Catholic CCD course at St. Joseph's Catholic Church in Columbia, they were studying the bible and had taken up David and Goliath. Billy really liked the name 'David,' so we named the infant boy 'David Gunnar Schachte.' The name Gunnar came from my Aunt Jree's husband, Gunnar Erickson."

Schachte continued to take an interest in law and applied his abilities as best he was able to succeed in the classroom. He found that the process and reasoning for applying the law became clear and meaningful. The courses were demanding, and the work outside of the classroom was intense. Many students left the program. Being older and married with a second child supplied the motivation. He completed the coursework with a new sense of preparation and organizational ability. He graduated with honors.

The young naval officer now had a new word to place behind his name, "Esquire." The law degree would change the course of his naval career.

"After law school and the passing of the South Carolina Bar exam, I was transferred to the JAG Corps and assigned to the Navy Legal Service Office in Charleston, I was hoping to go to other commands, but there were no transportation funds available at the time. As it turned out, that was another lucky break because of family commitments," Schachte explained. "I had lost my dad shortly before I started law school, and it allowed me to spend time with my mom and other members of my family who lived in Charleston."

Schachte's legal expertise within the Navy was becoming a favored asset. He would be called back to Virginia and then to Washington.

"I was later transferred to Norfolk, Virginia, and served as number two in the legal office of the Commander of Naval Surface Force Atlantic and my immediate JAG (Judge Advocate General) boss there eventually became an admiral, Don Campbell. We were dealing with 156 ships, and, in order to accommodate their legal requirements, I would work every Saturday. On Saturdays, I could deal with the executive officers of the ships up and down the east coast that were in the port and not interfere with their normal work schedules. They often had seemingly endless legal matters to resolve," Schachte detailed.

Eventually, the law would take him to a higher level of capabilities essential to the global reach of the United State Navy.

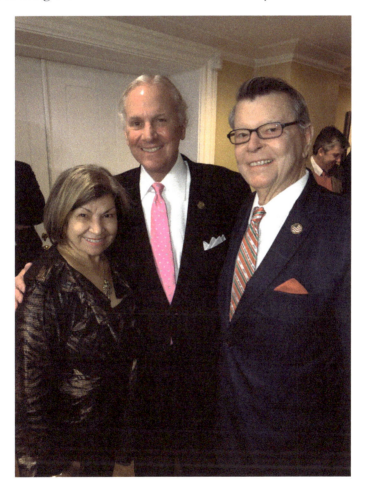

Carmen and Bill Schachte with friend, South Carolina Governor Henry McMaster. McMaster and Schachte were South Carolina School of Law classmates, graduating in 1973. Photo courtesy of Schachte Family Archives.

CHAPTER 11
International Law Expertise

Two middle-aged brothers took their wives on a Mediterranean Sea cruise to visit the exciting ports-of-call. The siblings stood at the rail surrounding the pool deck, drinks in hand, looking west across at a magnificent sunset.

The older sibling wistfully said to the younger, "I never contemplated that the Med was so wide. There is no land in view anywhere. It's just water as far as the eye can see."

The younger sibling, noting the opening for humor, stopped and took a sip of his drink. He supposed the older brother was waiting for an intellectual insight to capture the moment. He stumbled upon something timely to reply.

"It's true that all we see in every direction is water glimmering in the low sunlight. And can you believe that's just the top of it? There's much more below what we see."

In the lighter moment, there was an insight. Who is in charge of the surface (transportation), the depth (mining and oil rights) and what's in between (fish and submarines)?

"International maritime law would appear to be the simplest concept accorded the world's largest surface area. It is not quite so. Somebody has to make the rules. The United Nations is the accepted authority. We know the complexity of the 'law of the land.' The sea has some controversy that arises all-too-often," Schachte confirmed. "Laws are universally breached."

It is on the land that the lawyers, the plaintiffs, the defendants, the bailiffs, and the judges schedule backed-up logs of litigation by county, state, and district. The law of the sea still has cases pending in those same land-side courts around the globe.

Admiral Schachte earned his place among the world's elite intellects in the matters of the waters. It was his primary expertise.

To be sure, maritime law was not all he did. Schachte earned numerous military decorations to include the Defense Distinguished Service Medal and the Navy Distinguished Service Medal. In the rarified air of other accomplishments, he earned the Defense Superior Service Medal, two Legions of Merit, the Bronze Star with the Combat "V", the Combat Action Ribbon and the Vietnam Service Medal with one silver star. He also earned the prestigious Republic of Vietnam Meritorious Unit Citation—the Gallantry Cross Medal (color with Palm).[62] The man had done much in service to the country.

His abilities meant that he would be called upon often when those aqueous conflicts bubbled to the surface. Among his most memorable occurred on the home island that produced his lifelong companion, Carmen. He was called to resolve a deepening conflict in Puerto Rico.

"When I got to the Captain's office, he told me that I was going to be sent to Puerto Rico to assist those who were assessing the situation. It had become almost totally political. As it turned out, that is exactly what it was–politics in action. I then was asked to contact the number three person in the JAG Corps chain-of-command, Captain John Jenkins. Captain Jenkins eventually became an Admiral. At his direction, I was calling him every afternoon with the latest on what had transpired. I was sent down to Puerto Rico on orders to be there for a short period. The timing did not stay that way.

"After I was working on the situation, I was told they were going to send me to Puerto Rico in blocks of additional duty of three months at a time.

"The political problem concerning the use of the Island of Vieques in Puerto Rico came to the forefront. Vieques was a Naval gunfire support range that became front-page news. I was quite familiar with that island. On my first ship, I was a gunnery officer, and we used to perform target practice on Vieques. It looked like the local folks in Puerto Rico were going to insist on closing that firing range, which was a very necessary part of Naval Surface Force training. I was called into the office of the Senior JAG at CINCLANT Fleet in Norfolk."

CINCLANT refers to the Commander-in-Chief of the Navy's Atlantic Fleet.[63]

"Of course, I had a sincere regard for the people of Puerto Rico. My wife's family had a significant role in my life. There were fishermen there at Vieques that made a living from the waters surrounding Vieques." Schachte had a sensitivity to their plight.

A portion of Vieques Island, fifty-two square miles, had been a Navy firing range since 1938.[64] A territory of the United States, the exercises—specifically the Navy firing range—incited protests from the Puerto Ricans seeking independence.

"Though the law was on our side, we lost the use of the island firing range politically. I knew the result would be that the Feds would close down the military base on Puerto Rico—Roosevelt Roads. I tried to guide the conversation to that conclusion to actually help the Puerto Ricans. I sensed the long-range implications," Schachte explained. "But sometimes the loudness of the protesters will supplant good judgment."

As Schachte implied, the Roosevelt Roads military base closed with the subsequent loss of 2,000 Puerto Ricans jobs—a significant impact upon the local economy.[65] Other smaller military facilities closed, as well. It left the United States with only one naval base in the Caribbean—at Guantanamo Bay on the island of Cuba.

Entrance to Naval Station at Roosevelt Roads, PR. The Vieques Island resolution had grave impact to the established naval base. Photo Courtesy U.S. Navy.

"As a legal person, you argue the law—but as a human being, you must adhere to a sense of decency. Unfortunately, my points fell on deaf ears," Schachte intimated. "I felt bad for those island families who were now desperate for work."

Schachte was at another crossroads. In Navy terms, he was between a storm and an approaching enemy force.

"During the long negotiations, I requested reconsideration for my assignment in Puerto Rico because I had applied and been accepted into the master's program in International and Comparative Law at the George Washington University Law School," Schachte revealed. "I was given the consideration and began the master's program."

"Captain Jenkins intervened and directed that I continue with those plans to transfer from the Norfolk area to the Washington area to begin studies in the master's program. That was a significant and career-changing break." He divulged.

Schachte was relieved to have the opportunity and support.

"I thoroughly enjoyed that year in the program—with full pay and allowances. I learned a lot just by observance in D.C. It seemed like almost all of the courses had guest lecturers from the D.C. area who had been working on matters that we were studying at the time. I graduated first in my class, and I was sent immediately to the Pentagon. That was the start of my twelve years of service inside the Pentagon," Schachte smiled. "Higher education carries you to places that can be most beneficial, and at the same time, most interesting."

He completed the master's program at George Washington University in 1979.

With his advanced law degree in hand from George Washington University, Schachte found his stride in the understanding and administration of international maritime law. As his career progressed, Schachte's responsibilities in that arena grew. His later adjudication of international maritime law was outlined via the world authority, the United Nations. The laws are published for all nations in every language. He knew that publication much like he knew his personal Bible. It was his job.

Schachte spent much of his remaining career in the Pentagon. He became the Deputy Assistant Judge Advocate General (JAG) of the Navy in 1984.

By 1988, Schachte enjoyed the promotion to Rear Admiral, Lower Half. He earned his stripes. Two years later (1990) he was promoted again to Rear Admiral Upper Half. By 1992, his most accomplished legal level was attained—as the acting Judge Advocate General of the Navy. He had over 1,100 attorneys working under his supervision.

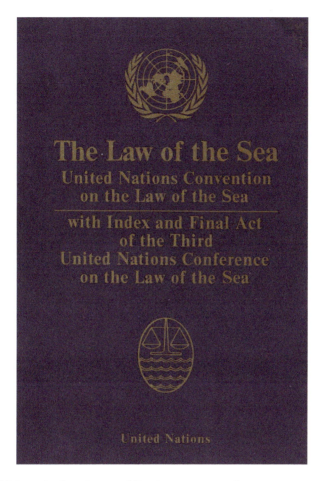

This United Nations publication serves as the quintessential reference to disputes of sovereignty upon the world's waters. Manual provided by Admiral W.L. Schachte, Jr.

Schachte's wide experiences resulted in his advancement. He became an expert on matters of maritime law and intelligence. He understood the world of spies—especially the Soviet effort to infiltrate U.S. systems and personnel.

After just a few years overseeing much of the international mediations and adjudications, his expertise would undergo a nearly-cataclysmic test. It would involve the Soviets. Tempers flared on both sides of the Iron Curtain.

Schachte, along with his negotiation team and state department officials were called to Geneva. The Soviets were at it again. The incident occurred on February 12, 1988.

The Black Sea is a cold place in February to begin a potential world conflagration.

"We operate globally on maritime law—which is not always accepted by some of the rogue regimes. The Soviets were known to be the worst of the perpetrators. A 'Right of Passage' is the standard," Schachte explained. "The Black Sea is recognized internationally as an open sea lane utilized by many countries for trade, fishing, and other mercantile interests in addition to military operations. Yet it has been among the most troublesome of the maritime oversight areas in the world. There are plenty of incidents that have emerged there over the years.

What is accepted in the restrictions of international maritime law is challenged repeatedly by other national interests of other nations—and possibly those interests of the United States.

International maritime law was codified in 1948 (and ratified by 21 countries in 1958)[66] by the United Nations to govern all nautical matters—especially commercial shipping. Since 1790 the U.S. Coast Guard has been the enforcer of U.S. maritime interests. But the UN set up another larger body known as the IMO (International Maritime Organization).

The IMO is headquartered in London.[67] They try to oversee everything over the sea. Common sense usually prevails, but not always. The ship's flag determines the source of the law as well as the criminal law of the ship's crew.

It is sometimes confusing. Schachte explained.

"For instance, the IMO, as part of the United Nations, has codified that international waters begin at twelve miles from any coastline. There are many extensions of their oversight to include controls for pollution, sewerage, and other harmful substances. These rules are made by treaties and conventions that propose to elevate all nations to the justification and adjudication of their purpose. The maritime laws are applicable to oceans and seas."

Billy Schachte had been called upon many times as the expert on the subject, even testifying before Congress. He had been called to testify on his expertise before the Senate Armed Services committee well after his retirement from the Navy (on April 8, 2004) to discuss the Law of the Sea Convention.

"Nothing in the Convention will affect the way we currently conduct surveillance and intelligence activities at sea. Opponents to the Convention argue that the Convention's provisions on innocent passage–Articles 19 and 20–will prohibit or otherwise adversely affect U.S. intelligence activities in foreign territorial seas at a time when such activity is vital to our national security. I can say without hesitation that nothing could be further from the truth," Schachte testified.

There were concerns raised about how other countries interpreted maritime boundaries. Schachte followed the activities and was often called to conferences to speak on these matters. His abilities in the area of maritime law were considered exceptional. His testimony served as a warning to the changing view of countries impacted by maritime rights.

The US Senate refused to ratify the treaty. He explained the dynamics to the full Senate Committee on the record.

"I think it is also important to note…that not everyone agreed with our 'customary international law' interpretation announced by President Reagan in his 1983 Ocean Policy Statement. However, our ability to influence the development of customary law changed dramatically in 1994 when the Convention entered into force. As a non-party, we no longer had a voice at the table when important decisions were being made on how to interpret and apply the provisions of the Convention. As a result, over the past 10 years, we have witnessed a resurgence of creeping jurisdiction around the world. Coastal States are increasingly exerting greater control over waters off their coasts and a growing number of States have started to challenge US military activities at sea, particularly in their 200 nautical mile (nm) EEZ."[68]

The acronym EEZ refers to "Exclusive Economic Zone." Some countries interpreted this zone as extending out to two hundred miles from their coast.

The retired admiral's insights became essential to modern maritime administration—especially as it incorporated the interests of the United States.

His post-military career as a maritime expert evolved with important contributions to the subject at seminars and in governmental chambers.

CHAPTER 12

The Pulse of the Pentagon

Schachte's legal career in the study of maritime law would become beneficial to his burgeoning career. His move from Norfolk to the Pentagon brought both career advancement and the enhancement of his specialized international legal training. Maritime navigation law evolved in the 1970s and 1980s and the United States became the reference authority. "All in all, I spent about twelve years in the Pentagon on various assignments in the Office of JAG and also in the Office of the Secretary of Defense. While in JAG, my first assignment was head of the Law of the Sea Desk in the International Law Division. By that circumstance, I was assigned to the U.S. Delegation of the Law of the Sea Conference. We had sessions at the Palais de Nations in Geneva for six weeks, and then later, I was posted to the United Nations.

"I spent eight weeks in the final session of that Law of the Sea Conference at the U.N. One hundred and fifty-seven nations participated in that conference. My participation was a tremendous experience which I cannot ever forget," Schachte admitted. "One has to be versed in the subject and also open to new concepts while respectful of international custom and consistency concerns."

"One of my responsibilities while first assigned to the Office of the Secretary of Defense was working for JAG Admiral Bruce Harlow—a true hero to me and many others. My job was to provide legal guidance and coordination for proposed Freedom of Navigation Operations. We called that 'FON,' Schachte stated. "Using acronyms is a standard military practice that the public may find quite confusing at times."

"One might walk the halls of the Pentagon and hear nothing but acronyms. To the uninitiated, it's a distinct foreign language," Schachte confided.

The world depends on an impartial system for international matters.

"The United States has always taken a lead role in these discussions, as we are seen as fair and ecumenical by most countries," Schachte added. "Indeed, we've become the world's police of the open seas."

Schachte provided much direction on maritime matters to foreign governments out of his Pentagon office. International maritime law is both complex and highly contested by some nations—ostensibly the rogue powers. The Pentagon's oversight is critical to these and other multi-national issues.

The massive Pentagon complex was completed in 1943.[69] It houses the headquarter offices of three service departments—the Army, the Navy (which includes the Marine Corps), and the Air Force. The seemingly innumerable offices house more than 25,000 workers inside nearly 3.7 million square feet of floor space. It remains one of the largest buildings ever constructed in the world.[70]

*The United States Pentagon.
Photo courtesy of U.S. Government.*

"Admiral Harlow was the second admiral to be assigned personally by the Secretary of Defense as the Department of Defense Representative for the Ocean Policy Affairs or the acronym 'DODREPOPA.' I later became the third admiral to be so appointed by the Secretary of Defense as the Department of Defense Representative for Ocean Policy Affairs. In that capacity, we represented the Secretary of Defense and the Chairman of the Joint Chiefs of Staff in all matters relating to ocean policy. This representation included domestic and international maritime functions. We were involved in bi-lateral and multi-lateral negotiations," Schachte explained. "There were always segmented areas of expertise associated with the military purview in the Pentagon. We were those ocean experts."

"After I retired, that position started being turned over to whomever happened to be the judge advocate general of the Navy at the time. It made sense that these roles merged," Schachte opined.

The two-star flag officer had participated in several high-profile legal procedures over the dozen years in Arlington. Many situations had been brewing for a time internally before they exploded in sensational headlines.

He alluded to one that involved his legal acumen.

"There was a special operation that was designed to challenge (Libyan Dictator) Moammar Gadhafi's Line of Death going across the Gulf of Sidra in contravention to International Law. I signed off on the ROE (Rules of Engagement) with direct oversight of Admiral Harlow for that operation. The operation was conducted at night. Consequently, we bagged two Libyan fighter jets when they pursued our jets as our aircraft exercised the international rights of freedom of the high seas. Gadhafi tried to seal off the rights of passage from the rest of the world. He miscalculated."

The bombing of the Gadhafi tent (April 15, 1986)[71] required precise and coordinated military interaction. The U.S. meticulously planned and executed the airstrike. Gadhafi, who had been complicit in several terrorist attempts impacting United States interests, was not at the tent facility and escaped the precision assault. Schachte's knowledge of the air and maritime laws required that he be eventually involved. The aftermath of the attack made it to Schachte's desk in the Pentagon.

"To my amazement, Gadhafi—in one of his boisterous and blustery moments—put out what they called a 'hit list' of people who had harmed Libya. My name was on it as a Navy commander. I treated it more as a joke than anything else. This then-confidential information came forth via an officer who carried highly classified documents to selected officers in the Pentagon. I was surprised that anyone in Libya even knew that I existed," Schachte related.

"Sometime later in 1989, when I was in Geneva on the U.S. Delegation to the Law of the Sea Conference, one of the CIA agents assigned there came to the small office I was using at the U.S. Mission in Geneva. He informed me, in a quote that I will always remember, of the subsequent fallout. He said, 'Bill, I don't want you to get alarmed about this but there are two goons from Libya who had cleared Passport Control in Geneva yesterday. This being Switzerland, we don't think they will try anything stupid. But you should change your schedule. Ride a different bus to the embassy for breakfast before the convention sessions re-convene. Also, we know that you jog around Lake Geneva after hours a lot. You might want to alter that. Oh, by the way, if you happen to see me out in the city, don't recognize me, please. I know you are a very friendly guy. I don't want to hear, 'Hey, Fred.' These Libyans had tried to bully other countries in the region, and it seemed that they wanted to test the U.S. resolve.' The agent was on it. I was impressed by his professionalism but also concerned that the Libyan reach was that broad."

"The gentleman that warned the maritime law expert had a top security clearance. He was in Geneva for other classified purposes." Schachte stated.

"I am glad he said that because two days later I was in Geneva getting ready to head back to the hotel where I was staying. I saw him talking with someone in earnest in a kind of darkened space between buildings. I walked right by him, and we made eye contact. I did not utter a word. He seemed relieved. I asked him later—and yes, he was doing work for Langley at that very moment that I saw him—so it was a good thing that I didn't say anything to him," Schachte remembered.

Libyan dictator Moammar Gadhafi was killed by an uprising of other Libyans in the Battle of Sirta on October 20, 2011.⁷² Schachte was glad that he did not succeed in the fulfillment of his secret hit list.

"I suppose there may have been operatives trying to mark my travel outside of the US. I would also assume that I was not among their major targets," Schachte intoned.

Nonetheless, Schachte's experience broadened to intelligence operations.

Langley, Virginia, serves as headquarters for the Central Intelligence Agency (CIA).[iv] He would spend much time visiting that facility from his office in the Pentagon. His travels took him to unique and sometimes dangerous destinations around the globe. There seemed to be a regular trip to Geneva.

"While I was in Geneva, Carmen flew over to Paris on my nickel, of course. I arranged to get to Paris to meet her at the main airport – Charles De Gaulle. I wish I had a picture of her expression when she saw me standing at the foot of one of those enormous escalators. We spent time in Paris and later went to Nice on the French Riviera and stayed at my Uncle Henry's summer residence at Beaulieu Sur Mer for the weekend. We had an amazing dinner at the famous La Rèserve Restaurant there," Schachte remembered fondly.

Beaulieu Sur Mer is between Nice and Monaco on the French Riviera. Young Billy and brother David Schachte enjoy the respite with their Dad. The admiral's uncle, Henry Schachte, owned this residence in Beaulieu Sur Mer. Photo Courtesy Schachte Family Archives.

On another occasion, Schachte retold the circumstances of a planned trip to Central America.

"I was the Manager of the Freedom of Navigation Program in the Pentagon. This position required more coordination than anything else. Accordingly, I worked with the country desks in the Office of the Secretary of Defense for the various countries that might be involved with our operations. Likewise, I worked with the country desks of the Joint Chief of Staff group. When anything came up that could impact the international press, I had a contact for the White House. That individual was a Military Liaison to the President. The person who served that role was Marine Corps Lieutenant Colonel Oliver North.

"I came to know and respect Ollie during those days and weeks and got to know his secretary, Fawn Hall, because of the frequent interaction of our offices. At one point, Fawn contacted me and said that Ollie and a fellow from the State Department and another person from the NSC were flying down to the Gulf of Fonseca area. The Gulf of Fonseca is in the Pacific Ocean in Central America bordering El Salvador, Honduras, and Nicaragua. They wanted me to go as they were talking in terms of a potential blockade or interdiction operation. They knew of my Swift Boat experiences and also of my Law of the Sea background. I rationalized that whatever they were considering would involve that expertise," Schachte retold. "It had been a problem area, and I knew many of the details and motivations that influenced those countries at that time," he described.

"The Gulf of Fonseca is a different model in the Law of the Sea. It operates on a condominium theory of law where those bordering countries share individual and different maritime rights.

"After I was notified of the pending trip, I was told that we would be there for two or three days. We were going to fly down in an executive-configured C-9, which is an aircraft that holds four people and four executive type seats and fold-out desks from the bulkhead. A day later, Ollie North's secretary, Fawn Hall, called and told me, 'I'm sorry Commander, your seat has been taken by Mr. Phil Merrill.' Phil Merrill was the owner and publisher of *The Washingtonian* Magazine. He was a very wealthy person listed as a consultant to the Department of Defense under President Ronald Reagan."

Merrill was once the president of the U.S. Import Export Bank.[73] He died of very mysterious causes in 2006. He had held posts in six presidential administrations.[74]

"I thanked her and didn't think much more about it," Schachte retold. "Months later, I needed to go over to see Ollie on a pending maritime-related operation. I went to his old office in the Old Executive Office Building. It was vacant. So, I asked around, and I was told that he was on a different floor. He was in a secured space. I went to that office and was unable to get in because there was a cyber-electric lock outside on the wall by the door entering the office spaces. I pushed the buzzer, and Fawn answered. She told me that Ollie was not available and that he was not in the building. If I really needed to see him, I should call her back, and she gave me a number to their secure phone. It was the same number as I had used before. I deduced that something or some incident had changed the status of his accessibility," Schachte concluded. "I had no idea how big that incident was to become. And, unwittingly, I was nearly a part of it."

Marine Corps Lieutenant Colonel Oliver North testifies before Congress. Photo courtesy U.S Marine Corps.

"As it turned out. I never went into that secured office space with Ollie. I did what we had to do on a separate unrelated matter by a secured phone. So, when all the news broke about the situation that Ollie was involved in (Iran-Contra), I really had to pause and take a deep breath. I was thankful that I could have been drawn into a real difficult situation—while still not knowing to this day what had transpired on that trip. It was fortunate that my seat was taken," Schachte related. "And that may be an understatement!"

The Iran-Contra Affair plagued the last two years of the Reagan presidency. When the details of the deal that exchanged American weapons for the release of hostages in Lebanon along with Iranian cash to be used to support the anti-communist Contras in Nicaragua against the Sandinistas, there were many questions. Congress had specifically prohibited this type of arrangement, and an eight-year investigation ensued. Some officials were found guilty and others were absolved. Some escaped prosecution. It is unclear that the president, Ronald Reagan, had full and complete knowledge of the illegal three-way negotiation between countries. Reagan was never formally charged in the incident and his wide popularity was not impacted by the events and later, the hearings.[75]

Reagan explained his actions in his autobiography, *An American Life*, published in 1990.

President Ronald Reagan served from 1981 to 1989. Photo courtesy UPI.

Reagan reported, "It was only later when the Tower Board and Congress completed their investigations, that I learned that some on the NSC staff had gone farther to help the Contras than I was aware of...When I inquired about this, I was told the reports were inaccurate."

The incident would have gone unnoticed. However, an airplane was shot down over Nicaragua in 1986 carrying supplies to the Contras. Though Reagan said that he was told that the plane did not have American ties, the opposite proved to be true.[76] An apology was issued on television to the American people by the president.[77]

Ronald Reagan served as the American President from 1981 to 1989.[78] His post presidential years were hindered by the onset of Alzheimer's disease. He died in 2004.

What was abundantly clear was that the National Security Council (NSC) conducted the three-way negotiations. All leads pointed to the office of Lt. Col. Oliver North, a Marine Corps infantry officer who worked at the Pentagon. North had gained an excellent reputation for results in his pursuit of the terrorists who bombed a Marine Barracks in Lebanon (1983), killing 299 Marines. He assisted in the planning of the invasion of Grenada (1983) and the bombing of Libya (1986).[79]

The episode was counter to the president's declared stance of 1985— "The Reagan Doctrine.[80]" The doctrine specified that the United States of America should never negotiate for hostages. History is hazy in its portrayal of what degree of information that President Reagan knew and did not know.

"Another aspect of my Law of the Sea assignments was the fact that it required a significant amount of international travel. I enjoyed that benefit—although it was always coach travel. It was no frills and tight seating. It was what we all did. But in my travels, I learned a lot about different cultures. One stark example of this came about when I was on a three-person team to Jakarta, Indonesia, to talk with the Indonesians about their pending archipelagic claim.

"Under international law, there are specific land-to-water ratios along with limits on lengths of baselines and sea lanes for transit. Indonesia, being an island nation, was going to submit a claim for archipelagic status under the International Law of the Sea Convention. We had made several other stops on that trip. One of our stops was at the Solomon Islands—the capital of which is on the Island of Guadalcanal—a historic battlefield of World War II in the Pacific. Few would return to see this remote and distant island after the war, so I felt privileged to be there. It is where so much American blood was spilled during the war of the Pacific," Schachte stated.

Schachte extolled the achievements of those brave souls who conquered the islands on their way to defeating the Japanese Empire. "I had a patriotic feeling about Guadalcanal and was glad that I had that experience."

"By the time we got to Indonesia, the person who normally handled all of the speaking, the ambassador from the State Department, had a horrible cold. It was so bad that he could hardly talk. When we got to Indonesia, we were talking with the ambassador, and Bryan Hoyle told him that he could barely get out a sentence. His voice was at a whisper. He indicated to the ambassador that I was going to be doing all the talking. He was very comfortable with that. We were getting ready to leave the ambassador's office, and he turned to me to say, 'Bill, don't forget the drink.' I stopped in my tracks as we all did. I came back and sat down and said, 'Drink? What do you mean by that?' He said, 'Indonesia is the land of the indirect,' so everything is about saving face. The ambassador further explained the culture, especially the way that these meetings are usually conducted.

"He said, 'You will not be meeting with an official of the government. You will be meeting with the Prime Minister's brother, who is a big banker here in Jakarta. His offices are inside the bank that he owns. If all things go well at the meeting, your host will indicate that he was not being a very good host, or words to that effect. He'll then say that it is time to have some refreshments. That is their way. By the way, Bill, if things aren't going well, you will not be offered refreshments. That will be your signal that things are going poorly. In that case, the meeting should be adjourned.' The ambassador knew their traditions well.

"I thanked him for that, and he strained to add, 'Further, if that offer does occur, then that is a very good sign, but do not touch your drink whatever it is. In a Muslim country it won't be alcohol, of course, but don't touch it until your host invites you to enjoy it. That is another signal that things aren't going well, and that is a sign it should be adjourned.' After the detailed explanation, we got up to attend the meeting."

Schachte continued the odd cultural negotiation story.

"Sure enough, as the ambassador suggested and after about forty-five minutes of talks, our host said, 'Oh my gosh, how impolite of me! Would you care for some refreshments?' And he arose.

"We all indicated 'yes,' and so they served everyone. I had a Coca-Cola with one cube of ice. We began talking again, and our host was asking me some technical questions. As we were getting into those discussions, the more we talked, the more I glanced at my Coke in the glass and noticed that the one cube of ice was slowing disappearing. At one point our host said, 'I am really embarrassed. Let's enjoy our refreshments.' So, we quickly downed whatever we had in front of us. Some had coffee, and some had Coke or water. We got back to the U.S. Embassy, and I went in to debrief our ambassador. He smiled and told me that one of his people, a guy from the ambassador's office who accompanied us to this meeting, had already informed him that things went extremely well."

Schachte had traveled a long way to earn a positive result.

"The ambassador congratulated us on that meeting result. I, at that point, thanked Brian Hoyle because we would have blown the whole thing sky high had he not told us about the traditions expected in the offering of refreshments. We would have downed those things right away as soon as they were served—as we would do in the States. The ambassador was sharp, and he talked us through that one."

But there were many other international maritime negotiations. Schachte recalled a very odd one on another Pacific island.

"Once in Papua, New Guinea, our host served us some sort of drink out of a large vat that was non-alcoholic. It was some sort of water with some actual ground dirt from the area where we were. You were supposed to clap twice, take a sip of it, and then pass it to the person next to you. They were supposed to clap twice take a sip and pass it until everyone who were involved in the talks had a sip of this stuff. It didn't taste so bad, and I had a real tiny sip when it got to me. As I told Carmen, 'When in Papua!' That was quite an experience."

The Freedom of Navigation Program had attracted much interaction with the various affected countries.

"One of the other incidents that gained international attention was the Black Sea bumping incident. In attempts to diffuse that potentially dangerous situation as it developed, I was one of several who began meeting informally at 'a technical level' in a series of discussions with the Soviets. These meetings took place in DC and Moscow.

"The first informal meeting that we had took place in my home in Falls Church, Virginia. We were told by the State Department that they did not have any available Rep Funds (Representational Funds) available from the State Department. Upon hearing this and knowing that we would be engaged with the Soviets in a day-long meeting, I volunteered to host both sides in my home and asked for permission to get clearance. I obtained that clearance from the Defense Department and the State Department. I was able to get the State Department to provide an invitation which I gave to the head of the Soviet delegation a fellow I believe was called Rubikov," Schachte retold.

"At the beginning of our first day, I presented the invitation to the Soviet gentleman. He thanked me very much after reading it and said that they would be delighted to comply and then he asked me, 'What was the normal protocol?' I explained to Comrade Rubikov that it was just a casual meeting with drinks and some hors d' oeuvres. He looked at the invitation, and he said, 'I see it starts at 1800 (6:00 p.m.). How long should we be there?' I suggested they should probably leave by around 9:00 p.m. That would be appropriate. The next day, promptly at 6:00 p.m., a van pulled up in front of my house with the Soviet diplomatic license plates on it and the Russians who were attending piled out. Rubikov was in front, and they all came into my home. It was just Carmen and me at home," Schachte recounted. "It was an odd meeting in every sense."

The Schachtes were the American hosts to the Russians at a time when Cold War tensions were at a peak.

"None of my colleagues from the U.S. side had shown up yet, so I brought the Soviet Russians back to my deck and showed them my backyard. I was scrambling in my mind about how I am going to entertain these folks. It was awkward. Mikhail Gorbachev had recently taken over the Soviet leadership. That event prompted a discussion about whether they should drink alcoholic beverages. As was traditional for hosting events, I then invited them to enjoy some libation. I explained that I had orange juice, water, beer, or alcohol. Rubikov immediately said, 'Yes, Bourbon. One cube of ice, please.' The conversation became more relaxed after that. They all started drinking. Interestingly, our intel suggested that we try to find out who among those Soviets had been in Cuba. That became an easy chore because before they left, two of them started serenading my wife by singing '*Besame Mucho*.' Of course, Carmen knew this song."

Besame Mucho remains a very popular romantic ballad of the Caribbean, especially popular in Cuba.[81]

"They had gotten into their cups quite a bit. But before everyone left, we were all in my den and Comrade Rubikov was regaling us with these humorous stories of his days of assignment to the Soviet Mission in New York and at the U.N. He spoke about what they would do to try to avoid getting caught after traveling more than the allowed mileage distance away from New York City. They spoke, as required by protocol, all in innocent humor. At 9:00 p.m., the Soviet Ambassador stood up immediately and said to his delegation, 'It is time to go, men.' They all popped up and got ready to take off. That is when two of them sang *Besame Mucho* to my wife," Schachte smiled at the remembrance.

We were trying to establish the universally recognized international law as the precedent over the usual Soviet belligerence," Schachte said. "We began down a stern negotiation road with the promise of cooperation from the simple gesture of having them visit my home."

Results would come.

"It was a fruitful event and later, our Secretary of Defense, Caspar Weinberger, who was in China at the time inserted in one of his books that technical level talks had occurred with the Soviet Delegation and a Navy Captain, as I was at the time. The citation referenced that I hosted them in my home.

Schachte pointed out that there was an internal inconsistency.

"In fact, Secretary Weinberger did not like the hosting episode at all. He sent out a message to the Defense Department stating that until the Soviets apologized for the death of Major Arthur Nicholson, there would be no social intermingling. Fortunately, I had received permission from all those concerned that it was a technical level meeting although their side was chaired by an ambassador.

That recent (1985) Berlin report that Weinberger cited was troubling.

"Major Arthur D. Nicholson, Jr., 37, a member of the U.S. Military Liaison Mission in Potsdam near East Berlin that has monitored Soviet and East German military activity since the end of World War II" was mistakenly shot twice while crossing the border. "Nicholson, a Russian linguist, died of chest wounds." The guards did not offer assistance, and the major bled to death.[82]

"I was advised of the situation upon Secretary Weinberger's return by my dear friend who was working in his office, Lieutenant Colonel Rich Higgins. Later and tragically, Rich was transferred from the Pentagon to an assignment in the Middle East. Apparently, word got out of what his last assignment was, and he was captured by some enemy forces and executed. It was a profoundly sad situation. His wife was also a Marine Corps officer," Schachte recalled. "There was so much trauma associated with our solemn duty to the country. Rich Higgins was a great guy. His loss was personally tough on me and everyone who knew him."

Schachte knew that there were many pockets of terrorism around the globe in addition to those countries with severe ideological differences like the Soviet Union. All presented daily threats.

"None of us were that far up the pecking order. We were just trying to resolve the technical and legal problems that we had with the Soviets. The next time we got together at the technical level was in Moscow. I was one of five people who went to Moscow to resume those technical-level talks. We were put up in the Sovietsky Hotel which was ordered to be built by Stalin at the end of World War II.

"I had no idea that I would be there when something quite historical would occur," Schachte related.

The Legendary Sovietsky Hotel in Moscow. Photo courtesy Associated Press.

"The purpose of the famous hotel was to house and accommodate diplomats who were visiting Moscow after World War II. It is an elegant building with huge marble stairways. When we checked in, we were told by the receptionist—a lady of much girth—that we could have breakfast served in our rooms the next morning, if desired. We all opted to have the delivered-to-the-room breakfast. We asked that the breakfast be delivered to our rooms at 7:00 a.m. because a Soviet Foreign Ministry car was meeting us at 8:00 a.m. for our first meeting. We had already decided to meet for dinner after checking in. We went to the restaurant in that beautiful hotel and ordered a meal for the five us. The waiter took our order. We were having beef stroganoff, and our waiter went into the kitchen and came back out about five minutes later and advised they only had enough food for four of us. We had the four orders split into five.

"The next morning, there was no breakfast delivered to any room. So, the junior guy in our group who was from the JCS (Joint Chiefs of Staff), a naval JAG officer, went down to the front desk to check on our order. He came back to my room, laughing saying he had asked the lady what had happened. She said no breakfast because the phone on her desk was not working so she could not call the kitchen to place the order. She called it, 'a very pity.' Why it did not occur to her to get up from her desk and walk into the kitchen and give them the order was not understood. Our car came, and we took off for our next set of talks. They lasted all day. We were at a safe house—as they call it—a building that belonged to the Soviet Foreign Ministry but not housing any of their diplomatic people," Schachte established.

The Soviets kept a close eye on the visiting Americans.

"That evening they took us to the Bolshoi Theatre for a ballet. We met their car at the hotel and went to the ballet, and at intermission, we were invited to a special room which was usually reserved for government officials. They served us caviar and shots of vodka and other light hors d' oeuvres. Before we left, the head of their group suggested it would be easiest for us to catch the subway back to our hotel. There was a subway station right underneath the Bolshoi, and we were to get off at the stop by the soccer stadium. They showed us what that would look like in Cyrillic. We had a grand time at the Bolshoi and left as directed to get off at the subway exit that they indicated. We walked up the street level." Schachte described what he saw next.

"It was amazing," he recalled. "Tanks were going down the street and trucks full of soldiers. We thought it was a dress rehearsal to one of their big November celebrations. But it was in August. We were standing there trying to decide whether or not to rush across the busy street because the hotel was on the other side. Finally, a big Soviet 'zil' limousine pulled up right across the street from us and some guys with overcoats, their collars up, and wearing dark hats pulled low over their eyes got out. They looked like they had walked right out of an MGM movie production. We assumed that they were KGB. They looked straight over at us, staring at us strangely. We decided to get across the street somehow and get back into the Sovietsky Hotel. We did so and were not halted or shot at, so I guess those men decided we were okay. Looking back, I think they knew that we shouldn't be observing what was going on that evening.

"I went to sleep that night with the sound of tanks rumbling in the road outside on that big six-lane street. It wasn't until two days later when we got to Norway to provide a NATO back brief that I learned what had happened. That was the night that there was an attempted coup on Gorbachev. It did not succeed. We were in the middle of something colossal and didn't know it," Schachte detailed. "Of course, we knew not to ask anyone about the sudden show of strength that evening in Moscow."

The August 1991 coup was disorganized and stopped short of removing the Russian leader. When Russian president Boris Yeltsin sided with Gorbachev, his popularity rose. Yeltsin would soon become the new Russian leader. The George Bush presidency, embroiled in the Gulf War of 1991, chose not to become involved in the outcome of the attempted coup.[83]

"Honestly, we never felt very safe while in the Soviet Union. Bizarre things could happen. We always felt that we were being watched. Once we cleared Soviet airspace, there was a sense of relief. Some of the fellows just went straight home. The other State Department person who accompanied me on the flight to Norway for the back brief felt as I did about the Soviet visit. It was best to do our job without incident and leave promptly.

"I had brought a new camera, a Minolta, on the trip to Moscow. When we got to Norway, my hotel room was on a corner area and it was a beautiful street scene of cars passing by. It was snowing very lightly, and I thought I could get a time delay shot with my camera. I opened my suitcase where I had packed it, and it was not there. After I got back to the Pentagon, I called the Naval Attaché and thanked him for the hospitality and told him about my camera disappearing. He simply asked me, 'Bill, did you pack your camera in your luggage that you checked in at the airport?' I said, 'Yes sir, I did.' He said, 'That was not smart. That camera was on the black market before your plane left the runway.' It was a lesson learned. It was my first chance to test the sentiment, 'Trust, but verify.' I trusted that my camera would be in my luggage—but didn't verify."

Progress was made to achieve a purpose. Schachte's skills in these matters made a difference.

"Our initial discussions with the Soviets eventually resulted in 'The USSR-USA Joint Statement on the Uniform Interpretation of Rules of

International Law Governing Innocent Passage,' signed by Secretary of State James Baker and Soviet Foreign Minister Edward Shevardnadze on September 23, 1989.

"I served as Deputy JAG and Commander, Legal Service Command from 1990 to 1993. After receiving my second star, I became the Deputy Judge Advocate General of the Navy and the Commander of the Navy Legal Service Command responsible for all the law officers around the world. Shortly after that, the Gulf War began. One of the Navy Legal Service Command's larger offices was in Naples, Italy. The commanding officer, Captain Rick Schiff was a dear friend and one of our best commanding officers. Rick called me in my office at headquarters and asked me to consider going to Naples because they had a number of his attorneys deployed on ships that were engaged in the Gulf War. All but one of the law officers were married, and their wives were very nervous about their husbands being deployed in combat zones." Schachte explained the situation.

There was a reason that it was important for Schachte to go to Naples.

"Since I had spent a year on Swift Boats in Vietnam running rivers, Rick thought it would be good if I could get permission to travel to Naples and talk to all the wives. I could give them encouragement and explain how my wife Carmen coped during the year I was in Vietnam. I thought it was a great idea and immediately set out to get clearance to travel, which was very difficult at the time. I finally received permission to travel under several conditions. Number one, I had to fly military air at all times while in the European theatre. Secondly, I could not be seen in uniform at any time during the day while I was in the Naples area, and as a part of that plan I was to stay with Captain Schiff and their family in their quarters. Additionally, I was advised to not ride in any government vehicles," Schachte recalled. "It was a tenuous experience."

Americans in the Middle East are usually easy to spot.

"My aide at the time was Bill Sweeney—a very competent and good attorney--and a good man. Sweeney was a prominent red-headed Irishman—a fact which became even more noticeable after we left the middle east theatre via the commercial airport in Heathrow. I was allowed to return to America on commercial air."

He continued.

"I stayed with Rick Schiff and his wife, Judi, and their children—and wore an overcoat over my uniform at all times. I traveled around in Rick's personal car—a rusted-out Fiat, a small car. I did, in fact, meet with all of the wives. I was told that the meetings went extremely well. The wives were reassured about the relative safety of their husbands. The extent of their actual exposure to combat was minimal. And in any event, they were serving our country," Schachte stated.

Schachte completed the intended mission successfully.

"Bill Sweeney and I flew by Naval Air to Heathrow. We spent the night in Heathrow and the next morning went to our flight going back to the States. It turned out that the plane was virtually empty. Some retired transit workers on holiday were on the flight along with Bill and me.

"Going through Customs, Bill was pulled aside and questioned about his possible involvement with the Irish. I, of course, stood up for him immediately, and we produced military identifications cards. They finally believed that he was indeed my aide and not an IRA guy undercover or anything else like that." Schachte retold.

With the perils evident for Americans in the Middle East, it was ironic that the only confrontation on Schachte's mission was because a man with reddish hair arrived in England. The world was rife with conflict.

"We boarded our flight back to Washington, DC. I was delighted to have made that trip, and I appreciated Rick Schiff. Schiff sadly passed away a couple of years ago."

Schachte's memory of the Reagan years (1981-1989) stood out.

"President Ronald Reagan was fond of the Canadian prime minister, Brian Mulroney. One evening after dinner in Canada's prime minister's residence, he showed the press a globe and pointed out the Northwest Passage over which they wanted to exercise control. By maritime law, it was a high seas corridor. But President Reagan agreed with the Canadian minister's push for control. When he returned to the White House, my boss in OSD got a call from General Colin Powell with instructions to make it happen," Schachte detailed.

General Colin Powell was President Ronald Reagan's National Security Advisor from 1987 to 1989, later becoming the Chairman of the Joint Chiefs of Staff under President George H. Bush.[84]

"The Navy staff was outraged. I had done a little work for General Powell when he was in the Pentagon. I was tasked to get word to him to express the polite outrage of senior Navy admirals. General Powell asked that I get the folks together for a meeting in the White House Situation Room which he chaired. I was invited and took notes so that we could try to forge a solution," Schachte recalled.

"The meeting started with a strong argument against the Canadian control from the Navy staff. They argued that the precedent would be alarming to others. Many countries, Indonesia especially, had sought such an accommodation of control.

"The Navy advised that we had requested permission in the past before transitioning Canadian waters and all were rejected or denied repeatedly. General Powell then shut it down saying the President had already decided and that we had to figure out how to make it happen," Schachte remembered. "There was no going back to the previous protocol."

Not understanding the global ramifications, the president would be causing a territorial waters uproar and a subsequent crisis that would reverberate in politically sensitive areas elsewhere. The offer to Canadian Prime Minister Brian Mulroney was ill-advised but had to be ameliorated carefully.

"My JAG buddies and I came up with a solution. Under the Law of the Sea rules, if a foreign country wanted to perform marine scientific research (the acronym is MSR), permission was required from the littoral (shoreline) country. So, I called my counterpart at the State Department and told him when going through the Northwest Passage we'd be doing 'MSR work' and would thereby be requesting permission. All agreed that this solution would 'pass muster.' We implemented it. All went well with the new solution. I even had other related discussions with the Canadian prime minister's legal advisor at the time, Lenny Lagoe. It worked for them, as well.

"All went well until, on a Saturday morning in November, I got a call at home that a Coast Guard Ice Cutter needed to transit the Northwest Passage. I was asked to find a Marine Scientist to put onboard so that we'd comply with the MSR qualifier. The ice breaker would be entering from the west coast. It took a while, but I located a scientist from a university out there who was able to take time off to perform some research that was, in fact, meaningful. Of course, I had some help available from the Secretary of State and, if needed, the White House. This passage problem didn't surface again because, after that Coast Guard situation, all knew what and how to achieve permissive passage," Schachte explained. "We were able to navigate around a promise so that there were no negative repercussions in other global waterways." Schachte explained.

Schachte's expertise would take him to remote areas of the globe over the remaining years of his military service. It was not because he knew those foreign lands. It was because he knew the waters.

Competition in the Marine Corps Marathon of 1980 took much disciplined training. Arlington Cemetery is in the background. He completed four marathons! Photo courtesy of Schachte family archives.

CHAPTER 13
After Impact: The Black Sea Resolution

The Black Sea is among the world's largest semi-enclosed bodies of water. It exchanges water with the Mediterranean Sea through the Bosporus Straits, and is nearly 750 miles across at its widest point.

Many of Eastern Europe's notable rivers drain into the Black Sea. Among the largest are the Danube, the Dnieper, the Don, the, Dniester, the Southern Bug, and the Rioni.[85]

It has a wide incidence of international waters and had an incident of major international impact.

Admiral Schachte became a key figure in the investigation and resolution of a Soviet warship side-swiping a U.S. warship in Black Sea waters considered "international" by IMO standards, but not by then-Soviet standards.

"The Rules of Navigation and Sojourn of Foreign Warships in the Territorial Waters and Internal Waters and Ports of the USSR," enacted by the Soviet Council of Ministers in 1983, acknowledged the right of innocent passage of foreign warships only in restricted areas of Soviet territorial waters in the Baltic, Sea of Okhotsk, and Sea of Japan. There were no sea lanes for innocent passage in the Black Sea.[86]

"The Soviets had their own rules without regard for the commerce and free passage of other nations on what are uniformly considered international waters," Schachte explained. "That does not mean that we don't use the world-accepted standards."

The United States, starting from 1979, conducted a freedom of navigation program as the U.S. government believed that many countries were beginning to assert jurisdictional boundaries that far exceeded traditional claims under international law. The program was implemented because diplomatic protests seemed ineffective. The U.S. actions in the Black Sea were challenged by the Soviet Union several times prior to the 1988 incident, but the bumping incident sent the Cold War Era to a new level of tepid. The incident became the reason Schachte was called in.[87]

"I was on my way to Geneva to meet the Soviets," Schachte recalled. "It would be a few years before the wall came down and tempers were raw. The right of innocent passage by international standards was not violated. But Soviet standards were rarely in conformity with International Maritime Law. They see their role as the international bully. That is precisely why we have to be strong and not give in. We don't."

Indeed, the US position was the UN position. Nonetheless, there would have to be a confrontation extended landside—in a conference setting—by a new agreement placed to avoid such senseless "fire-starter" incidents. The Soviets agreed to the Geneva meeting. Ronald Reagan was in the White House. He had the same distaste of Soviet bullying that was extended by Admiral Schachte's stoicism. That attitude was becoming ever-more-clear to Soviet leader Mikhail Gorbachev. Reagan's verve served him and the country well. And Bill Schachte was the admiral he needed to articulate the American intolerance of the Soviet bad-boy behavior.

The Black Sea has internationally accepted maritime delineations. Photo courtesy of author from Google Earth.

Schachte knew that the negotiations would be fiery and difficult. He represented his country well.

"As Commander-in-Chief, President Reagan was an incredible boost to our military mindset. He believed in us, and we certainly trusted him. As so often happens, politics plays a questionable role in decisions that have been made in the White House and Congress over our history. Reagan was different in that regard. You knew that he had your back. It made the duty of every military officer easier to comport."

Admiral Schachte was much like those he served in his career—straightforward and reactive to situations he had been trained to perform—at the helm, in the Pentagon, and while seated at the bench.

"Tensions were—at least temporarily—suspended. We had a productive meeting. But I knew and our team knew that whatever agreements we felt we achieved with the Soviets would be tested again and again. That has been their century-long history. It remains amazing to me how their representatives show up and sign something that is altogether meaningless because they know—and you know—they will not honor their commitments nor adhere to laws. That may have started with Lenin and Stalin. Their citizens trust no one. It's because their regimes are built on deception and duress," Schachte emphasized. "Not much has changed—even today."

It was not until later years that the United States intelligence agencies received critical insight to the Russian and former Soviet strategies.

Few people outside of the international intelligence agencies knew of the enormous influence of the Soviet Union in organizing America's peace protests during the Vietnam War. Their targeted funding was equally complicit.

Russian GRU[88] (Soviet Military Intelligence) defector Stanislav Lunev said in his autobiography that, "the GRU and the KGB (Soviet Civilian Intelligence) helped to fund just about every antiwar movement and organization in America and abroad," and that during the Vietnam War the USSR gave $1 billion to American anti-war movements—more than it gave to the Viet Cong! The Russian defector did not identify any organization by name. Lunev described this as a "hugely successful campaign and well worth the cost" to the Soviets in their quest to end the war by inciting American upheaval.[89]

This information, many years after the Vietnam protests, was a major revelation of the manner in which the Russians approach international matters. It has long been evident that the Russians have a long-term penchant for funding organizations in other countries to achieve a result beneficial to Russia.

For a time, tensions were reduced when the Berlin Wall came down in 1989. It was short-lived. Much of the distrust returned with the rise of Vladimir Putin as the Russian president.

CHAPTER 14
NIS—Naval Investigative Service

The year 1990 can be described as the results of a domino field standing on end in a sequence. Communism took its biggest hit. It was a difficult time to serve as the Judge Advocate General. The world seemed to change daily. The Soviet Union was unraveling. The Berlin wall had already been sledge-hammered to rubble.

"It was no time to drop our guard," Schachte warned. "I had been to Russia recently—in 1988 and 1992."

The admiral accepted the new responsibility of 1,150 special agents utilized to counter the new wave of foreign spying. That was to be expected since the Soviets took money from their military for use in espionage. Schachte's new role as head of the Naval Investigative Service would require an abundance of skills.

"Under the Soviet glasnost policy, their budgets were cut. So, where would they get information?" Admiral Schachte asked rhetorically.

Naval Criminal Investigative Service Designation

He and his staff already knew that answer. The Soviets would steal every tidbit of classified information they could develop by their enhanced cold war tactics. They would spy. Once Admiral Schachte took charge, he strategized the department resources for optimum results. He had command of a major technological and human resource entity that could change history for the better. It was a daunting task.

There were known confidentiality problems. The Soviets became the Russians by 1990, but their basic spy operations did not change. Many securities had been breached before the admiral's arrival. Estimates to replace stolen computer codes in the systems across intelligence agencies approached $100 million.[90] The Russian spy budget was believed to be more than $250 million by 2018.[91]

And the spy networks grew as the military forces and Soviet defense spending dwindled. One estimate reported as many as 1,300 KGB operatives working in the United States in 1985.[92]

The Navy and the Federal Government were not impervious to dramatic developments in the spy arena. There was the John Anthony Walker, Jr., revelation. Walker had spied inside the U.S. Navy for the Soviets from 1968 to 1985.[93] He recruited his son to do the same. A similarly damaging spying episode materialized in 1997—the infamous agent Aldrich Ames.[94] Ames worked for the Central Intelligence Agency.

These were particularly difficult revelations that meant that the Russians and other potential enemies were receiving frequent confidential details from inside the U.S. Navy headquarters and other key governmental sources.

"I assumed command of NIS as a one-star admiral in 1989," Schachte stated. "It was a daunting challenge."

The NIS is now the NCIS. They added "Criminal" to the title to read, Naval Criminal Investigative Service. In time, "NCIS" became a popular television series.

"When that occurred, I was the most junior admiral in the United States. I was Admiral Number 257. That was a good number to keep things in perspective. I might add at the time the Navy consisted of over 550,000 officers and enlisted men and women.

Departmental travel commitments increased, and other contacts with the Russians brought other suspicions.

"On a trip to Moscow in 1992, we stayed at a different hotel, a newer hotel closer to the Kremlin," Schachte recalled. "But you assumed that every move and every word is under Soviet surveillance."

"This was right after it had been discovered that the newly constructed American Embassy had been honeycombed with listening devices. After we got settled in our hotel in Moscow, we went over to the Embassy. While there, the naval attaché invited me to go with him to the new proposed American Embassy building still under construction. He showed me the incredible honeycombed areas of all those bugs. It was on this trip that I had a message for him, but I was instructed not to write it down anywhere or have any written correspondence about that issue with me or in my briefcase. After we settled in and had our first meeting in the embassy, we would then go out to a field which was fairly close to the embassy. There were park benches on either side. I was told that we would walk down the middle of that open field because the Soviet listening devices couldn't reach that far. We did that, and I conveyed my message," Schachte explained.

"Our talks continued to proceed on pace with the Soviets on the International Law of the Sea issue that we had under discussions and then returned to the United States. Before we left, we were hosted out to a Moscow dacha.[95]"

A dacha is a second home awarded by the government to someone, usually of importance.[96]

"We were taken out there in a Soviet government zil[97] car," Schachte remembered with a smile. "It was quite an experience."

A zil car is a Soviet government limousine used on private lanes to transport important officials and their guests outside of the main auto traffic.

"It was amazing. We got in the car, but we were cramped. The first thing I noticed was the heavy odor of gasoline. We also noticed that once the driver got over a little over 60 kilometers an hour, there was a decided wobble in the right front tire. But the car had traffic priority. We didn't feel like we were very important to the Russians based on the zil car condition.

"When we arrived at the dacha, we noticed that the grass and lawn in front of the place looked shoddy and needed to be cut. Inside it was a different world. The place was clean and spotless. We had a very nice luncheon meal and then they drove us back to downtown. We were told not to worry about our conversation. The host said, 'You could say anything you want because the driver only spoke Russian and wouldn't know what we were talking about anyway.' Of course, we were convinced that the driver was another instrument of their spy system. As soon as we got in the car to go to that dacha, I started cracking jokes. I had just heard a couple that were pretty new and funny. We all laughed out loud. But, so did our driver. So much for him not knowing any English." Schachte recalled.

"There were other obvious indications that we were being watched and even recorded. On a second trip in 1992 one of the members of our group gave a report. He was a lieutenant commander. On the first morning in Moscow he got up around 5:30 and went for a jog. He came back, as he told me, and took shower and then dried off and used the only towel that was in his room. He figured he could dry that towel by putting it over a high back chair. The chair was placed in front of a big mirror that was in his room. He had put the towel on the chair and was walking back to the bathroom when there was a loud knock on the door. A lady who worked for the hotel came in and moved the towel from the chair. She admonished him to 'never put anything on any chair.'

"It was obvious to him then that there was a camera behind that mirror," Schachte reported.

Schachte continued by explaining, "We knew always to be careful about anything going on in Moscow. In fact, it was a surprise that we were hosted on that last day at their famed Moscow Press Club. We were told by the Embassy not to eat any of the vegetables that they served with meals in a buffet line because they were not considered that safe to eat. Everything that one would eat in Moscow was suspect—not just the vegetables. Fortunately, that was the last of those trips to the 'worker's paradise' as we called it. It is not a safe place," Schachte related. "Even their citizens are skeptical of the government."

Over the years the admiral gained a keen perspective of his travels, especially to the Soviet bloc.

"During that 1992 trip, two new guys with our group were walking around downtown Moscow and started saying aloud, 'AUB (Alpha Uniform Bravo).' I asked, 'What the heck is that all about?' They said we were simply commenting about the architecture that was put in place after the Russian Revolution (1918). AUB was their acronym for 'another ugly building.' But that's no secret. There are no buildings that would inspire anyone walking around Moscow. It's dreary and solemn—not a happy place," Schachte stated. "It was always good to get back to America."

CHAPTER 15
The 60 Minutes Interview

The April 19, 1989 USS Iowa explosion was prominent in the Washington headlines. A comprehensive U.S. Navy investigation, in the opinion of many, did not go far enough or reach the proper conclusion. With the confidential assistance of the Federal Bureau of Investigation, Admiral Schachte felt that a full review of the forensics, the personnel, the procedures, and the ship's condition might lead to a different conclusion. He ordered a second investigation.

CBS's *60 Minutes* with Mike Wallace wanted to present the findings to a national television audience. *60 Minutes* was an established and well-followed Sunday evening series. Their focus seemed to be an attempt to expose this event as a preventable naval tragedy. The network decided to speak to someone with the Naval Investigative Service about the Iowa explosion.

Schachte was new to the desk he had assumed, but a veteran of the duty-first attitude he had always employed. He accepted the interview per Navy procedure, though he was not allowed to discuss many aspects due to an ongoing investigation. Typically, the media does not come on a schedule, so the interview could occur when they spontaneously appear. That strategy could give the developing story even more drama. However, this interview was scheduled.

"In accordance with Navy tradition, I became the commander of NIS (now NCIS) and was instantly responsible for everything that had taken place in my command before I got there. In this instance, it was the investigation of the explosion on the USS Iowa which resulted in nearly fifty deaths. It was a somber affair, and I had been briefed on the initial investigation, which was pretty well completed by the time I had assumed command.

"I was finishing up a required military course called Capstone when I got word from the Secretary of the Navy's office that Mike Wallace of *60 Minutes* was going to be doing a segment on the Iowa explosion and that the Secretary of the Navy had made me available for that segment. I knew very little about the Iowa, other than what I had read in the papers.

The Battleship Iowa was a transformed Navy ship with the keel laid in 1940.[98] It was built in Brooklyn prior to Pearl Harbor and the U.S. involvement in World War II. It was launched in August of 1942 and commissioned in 1943. The Iowa was first decommissioned in 1949.[99] The Navy found financial and Cold War reasons to recondition and recommission the ship twice. The last refurbishing and recommissioning took place in 1984.[100] It was decommissioned a final time in 1990 and is currently preserved as a museum at San Pedro, California (near Los Angeles).[101]

The USS Iowa's considerable role in World War II was highlighted by a secret mission. The then-state-of-the-art destroyer transported President Franklin Delana Roosevelt from Washington to Algeria and back to meet with Josef Stalin and Winston Churchill at the Tehran Conference (November 1943).[102] Roosevelt traveled this route in the midst of enemy submarine packs roaming the Atlantic. His accompanying staff included the Army Chief of Staff, the Secretary of State, the Army Air Corps Commanding General, and other key advisors. The Iowa returned the president to Washington on December 16, 1943, after a month-long journey.[103]

The destroyer's extensive service into the Pacific Theater, during the Korean conflict, and the Cold War made it the iconic destroyer of the mid-WWII era—aptly named the Iowa Class.[104]

The unsolved April 1989 explosion occurred during training exercises at Gun Turret Two. The behemoth battleship had 65 officers and 1501 enlisted men.[105] The disaster took the lives of forty-seven crewman. What went wrong and how it sequenced became as much speculation as innuendo. The facts of the incident had to be determined. The media angles and backstories were compelling. There were those that believed the explosion to be an intentional act. Other possibilities included an accident related to a gunpowder storage ignition.

Prior to Admiral Schachte's role at NIS, an investigation had concluded the likelihood of an intentional act, though the case was built on much innuendo. The media was not satisfied with the results.

CBS's *60 Minutes* saw it as an unsolved mystery.

"I contacted my office. I had been out of the office at a Capstone course which is required of all admirals and generals who are newly selected—part of the Goldwater Nichols Act," Schachte explained.

Capstone is a transition assistance program required by the Department of Defense for advancement of military officers to flag officer status.[106]

USS Iowa in a prior training mission near Puerto Rico
Photo Courtesy U.S. Navy Archives.

"I asked my executive assistant to send me information on the Iowa investigation. The answer was, 'Admiral we have boxes of that stuff. How many boxes do you want?'

"I said, 'Don't worry about it, there must be some executive summaries somewhere. Just have those available for me.' I went back and began studying those, and I had great faith in our investigators. They were all college graduates and dedicated, patriotic Americans doing some very difficult work. I made myself aware of the basic facts of the investigation.

"On the Tuesday prior, I was told that Mike Wallace was going to do the interview on Sunday—in five days. I could choose the venue. I selected my office which was in the Washington Navy Yard headquarter area. They told me that the interview would be Sunday morning at 10 a.m. I did my best to get ready by studying the history and circumstances related to the USS Iowa explosion. There was controversy wrapped within the circumstances. Because some believed it was fully accidental and yet others attributed the explosion as an intentional act by one of the crewmen, it remained a mystery. There were multiple investigations to discern the cause," Schachte stated.

Among the forty-seven crewmen who perished was a previously disciplined navy chief who some believed was complicit in an intentional act of sabotage. The interrogations and inspections were begun immediately following the incident. The Navy investigation eventually concluded that there was no supporting proof that the warship had been compromised.

The media was not convinced.

"I went for a jog the morning of the interview. I then drove to my command to find my parking place was occupied by a Cadillac limousine. The driver had the seat all the way back and sleeping. His mouth was wide open. I looked up to my office, and I could see from the street the lights were already on and people were walking around. They had come much earlier than the scheduled 10:00 appointment.

"I then called my executive assistant and directed several instructions. We wanted to be hospitable and efficient," he recalled.

"I had previously been given some media training which was very helpful. It is part of the protocol of the service not particular to the Navy. I wanted to make sure that I gave truthful answers without speculating on things that I did not know. The media seems to want to advance speculations to deliver a story with more drama. In investigations, we deal in facts. There is an art to an interview that the professionals—like Wallace—use to their advantage. They are very good.

"I had done media role-play previously as part of my training. I could recognize the leading questions that took the story away from the facts. I recalled much of that training. My role-play interviewer gave me several outstanding pointers. One was to always keep your eyes on where his eyes should be. They knew that there would be producers passing him notes, and there would be other distractions. So, if you start following everything that is going on with your eyes, you will look a little shady because they will film your eyes darting all over the place."

Schachte continued.

"I remembered these basic filmed media interview insights and even to maintain my posture. It was important to try to keep my answers within twenty-second soundbites. And, of course, if I didn't know an answer to a question, I was to simply say that. That part was easy because there were file boxes full of unknowns. I had no time to know all of the answers," Schachte admitted. "And on that point, I had no agenda, and the Navy had nothing to hide. We were performing at our best to get the facts and establish the cause."

He further explained.

"Typically, the media is after a sensational story before the complete investigation is submitted. Innuendo and speculation are often the worst route to follow in an investigation. Facts always matter," Schachte stressed.

The media kept the pressure on even though our NIS investigation was still assembling all details in the second investigation of the USS Iowa. Newspaper copy from Admiral Schachte's personal archives.

Some of the national media seek to make their sources look inept and even foolish. The admiral became a quick-study expert on handling interviews.

"It was during this time that my mother called. When I told her about the character assassination that the media was apt to publish in the midst of the investigation, she sensed my frustration. Her answer to me was timely. She said, 'Calm seas don't make good sailors.' It was a brilliant response and one that I think about often when things go sideways." Schachte intimated.

"Indeed, the media can be deceptive. One of the media's tricks is to ask you a very simple question, to which they know you don't know the answer. It is so simple you realize that if you can't even answer that, you will not look believable to a television audience. They do these things intending to command the interview process. It's their camera, their producers, and their editors," Schachte reflected. "They have the million-dollar sponsors."

Schachte knew to be truthful and forthcoming but not at the expense of undermining an ongoing investigation. His allegiance was always to the integrity of the process that would determine the facts, and thus the truth.

"I was advised that the interviewer will have a clipboard in front of him at all times. Of course, I couldn't see what was on it. I was to stay fixed upon his eyes and the next question. The final thing they said was to accept the offer of makeup. There is nothing effeminate about that. But I was to insist upon it—since the process would only take a couple of minutes. The idea was to take the blandness and shine off your face. The visuals mattered. Properly briefed and understanding the seriousness of not getting ahead of the investigation, I felt that I was properly advised, and I felt I was ready," Schachte summarized.

He proceeded to his office.

"When I arrived, I went into my office, and I took my hat off and placed it on the hat tree. Someone from the news crew said, 'All right, Admiral please sit down here.' Mike Wallace was seated in the chair facing where I was. After introductions, he said, 'We have to take a break in thirty minutes to change the big reel of film that we have in the camera. So, if you can think of a question you would rather have answered differently, you can tell me about it when we break for that change of film. I will be glad to ask it of you again.' I was suspect. I had been briefed on the media's deceptions, though I felt that Mr. Wallace was being forthright. But I thought, 'Yeah, I know which answer you would use, too. It wouldn't be the second one it would be the first one.' I wanted to be certain to give my best and truthful answer each time. There would be no re-shoots.

"Mr. Wallace looked down and looked up at me, and the first thing he told me when we got started on the interview was, 'You're Admiral and I'm Mike.'

"I said, 'No, I'm Bill.' He said, 'No, you're Admiral and I'm Mike, do you understand that.' I said, 'Yes sir, you got it.' Then, I asked, 'May I go to the bathroom and comb my hair?' I had just taken off my hat. He said, 'Sure. When you come back, they will give you some makeup.'

"When I came back, they just powdered my face slightly. I sat down and they directed, 'Say 5,4,3,2,1. We want to set the sound right.' Then they said, 'Alright, go!'

"The interview began. I was told by Navy headquarters it was going to be a friendly interview. Of course, it turned out to be anything but. In fact, at one point before we broke at the thirty-minute point, I had our team rig a recording device in the room, so we would know exactly everything that was said.

"Mike Wallace starting out with a barrage of questions—tough ones that I either knew or didn't. I answered everything honestly and kept my timeline on twenty seconds or shorter. It was not like talking to me at a cocktail party. I was concise and directed. Then I shut up.

"He asked me a couple of seemingly obvious questions that I didn't know the answers to—but these may have been in those large file boxes, and he may have thought that I should know these answers. I told him, 'I am sorry but don't know the answer to that, but I will get back to you.' That seemed to upset him. But I did not want to give a speculative answer. If I didn't know the answer, I told him that."

Schachte continued to describe the experience.

"Then, at one point before the thirty minutes to change the film out, he looked down at his clipboard he had in his lap. His producers were handing him notes and doing all sorts of stuff throughout the whole interview, so that was good advice to me to focus on his face, regardless of where he was looking. He looked down a little and then in a very muted voice but one that all could hear, he looked at his notes and then up at me and said, 'A tough son of a bitch.' I heard it, of course, and we had it on our recording device. I looked up at him and said, 'You are right. This has been one of the toughest interviews in which I have ever been involved!' That made him even more upset. We did another thirty minutes. Nothing really changed," Schachte related. "I don't know who was more relieved that the interview was over—Mike Wallace or me!"

Admiral Schachte Hosts Journalist Mike Wallace of 60 Minutes. Photo Courtesy of Schachte Family Archives.

It would be a week before the edited version of the hour-long interview would be broadcast. The newly installed admiral felt confident that he had succeeded in being honest and forthcoming, though non-controversial and stoic.

"I didn't know how I had done until I saw a transcript of the interview the following day. That Monday, I was in Norfolk, Virginia, traveling with this Capstone Group, and we were meeting with Admiral Kelso, who was CINCLANT Fleet commander. I got the transcript from his office. After I read it, I felt good about it. We then left for the Pacific, with Capstone, and we got over to Hawaii on a Sunday. That was the day the program was airing. Since we were six hours behind, I called Carmen—who had seen the program back home in Washington," he recalled.

Schachte had no idea that Carmen had her own plan to deal with the national interview. She knew that a poor interview would likely short-circuit her husband's distinguished career.

"As an aside, on that previous Sunday when I came home after the *60 Minutes* interview, my house was dark. Carmen was away. I went upstairs to our bedroom, and I could see the flicker of a light and it as a holy candle. Carmen had been praying—and it worked well too. Believe me!" Schachte recalled.

The Schachte family prayer vigil is real. Carmen lit a candle and prayed for a positive outcome. Photo courtesy Schachte Family archives.

Schachte was unaware of how much of the film that the 60 Minutes interview would air in the segment about the U.S.S. Iowa investigation. He really didn't want to see too much of himself in "the crucible." He considered that less is better.

"There was ample time before the program was going to air in Hawaii. I called Carmen, and I asked her, 'How did it go?' She said, "You will be fine. Don't worry.'

"I said, 'No, how did it look?' " He asked.

"She said, 'Don't worry about it.' " Schachte recalled.

"So, I had to wait until I could see it in Hawaii time. And it was fine. I think I was on camera on this nationally-aired program about 26 seconds.

It was an answer to a question that he had asked about whether or not this person we felt was a culprit was going to be transferred to duty in England. We did not know if that was a fact. I told him that.

"He yelled at me about, 'You've got 158 special agents around the world and they are all college graduates and highly trained, and you don't know the answer to a simple question like that?' To which I said, 'That is correct, sir.' The experience was daunting, but I think I learned a lot about the media. And it's true that you have to become the controversy by your mannerisms and answers in order to expand the air time. It's good that they cut these things short."

Though the final determination of what happened to cause the tremendous explosion aboard the USS Iowa remains, in part, a mystery—much is universally known. The facts to include the incendiary materials, the burn temperatures, the time, the catastrophic effect, and the lost sailors are not for dispute. The interviews, the technology, the safety procedures, the crew interaction prior to and after the explosion leave much room for unproven speculation.

The Schachte family grown: L to R Frank, Margie, Billy, Kay and Joe. Seated "Aunt Jree" Erickson and mother Mary Schachte. Photo courtesy Schachte Family Archives.

In any set of circumstances, the catastrophe aboard the refurbished battleship was a devastation to the U.S. Navy of egregious proportions, but moreso to the families of those forty-seven sailors who perished. Admiral Schachte had been too close to military casualties in his career to not feel the pangs of its finality over and over again.

The USS Iowa incident brought about major improvements in Navy administrative investigations, especially in the case of any concern of intentional acts. That evidence has to be established clearly and concisely, without the cloud of unsubstantiated conjecture.

CHAPTER 16
Tailhooks of Intolerance

Operation Desert Storm had begun on January 17, 1991. The U.S. Navy executed their precision strikes impeccably. Their role in the engagement was lauded by high command and the White House. A meaningful portion of the air war activity depended upon the Navy's formidable strike and fighter pilots dispatched from aircraft carriers in the Persian Gulf and the Red Sea. These naval air professionals commanded fighter aircraft that had the distinguishing mechanical landing assistance from a hook under the plane's tail that caught a cable upon landing. It is called the "tailhook." Since 1956, these carrier pilots (including those flying carrier helicopters) have been meeting annually to celebrate their uniqueness and their service to the country.[107] They established a charitable non-profit and give annual scholarships to deserving students. The Tailhook Association has performed admirably in the service of the country and as a public entity helping others.

The 35th annual Tailhook Association meeting and symposium took place at the Las Vegas Hilton in September of 1991.[108] It was only eight months after the awesome display of airpower in Desert Storm. Things went horribly wrong.

Proper decorum was not followed at the convention. There was a leadership vacuum. Although this convention included the demographic change of increased female Naval aviators, planning for their inclusion was lacking. The female pilot assimilation was difficult for the Navy—and especially difficult for females who had chosen a naval career. Lt. Paula Coughlin, an admiral's aide—and helicopter pilot, brought the Tailhook Convention's atmosphere of misbehavior to the attention of her superiors. A contemporaneous *Newsweek* article described the circumstance.

Coughlin, 30 at the time, saw the group of Navy and Marine pilots hanging out in the third-floor corridor of the Las Vegas Hilton but didn't think twice about heading down the hallway. Then the terror began. Coughlin... hurtled down a gantlet of groping, poking and pawing officers, who grabbed her breasts and tried to remove her panties. "Help me," she implored a pilot, who then molested her too.

"It was the most frightened I've ever been in my life," Coughlin, the daughter of a retired navy aviator, told *The Washington Post*. "I thought, 'I have no control over these guys. I'm going to be gang-raped'.[109]"

The Post article cited other grave concerns.

"Even though scores of drunken officers assaulted at least 26 women, 14 of them officers, the navy initially treated Tailhook '91 as little more than a fraternity party that got out of hand. But with Coughlin's decision to speak out...the scandal took on a name and a face and finally began to resonate in high places. It had already become clear that senior officers knew behavior at the convention had gotten out of bounds but did nothing to subdue the aviators, and that many of the officers had refused to cooperate after the fact with two separate navy investigations.

Appalled by Coughlin's account, President Bush summoned Defense Secretary Dick Cheney for a briefing. Within hours, Secretary of the Navy Garrett tendered his resignation, which Bush—himself a former navy pilot—accepted.[110]"

As the investigation moved forward, it became clear to Coughlin and others—a total of ninety reported assaults to officers, enlisted, reserve and civilian victims—had not been satisfied with the investigation. It appeared that the assailants would not be fully exposed and brought to justice. The reported assaults were to eighty-three women and seven men. Lt. Coughlin and others demanded more. Unfortunately, the legal review and criminal prosecutions were both slow and ineffective. The lack of response became the second scandal.

Something had to change.

Admiral Schachte had been summoned to reopen and review the what was now a front-page cover-up, the Tailhook Scandal. He realized he had major interested parties— the White House, the Navy, women in the military, the media, Congress, and the American public. He needed to assemble a reliable plan of action that would be transparent, diligent, and effective. The assailants would be brought to justice.

[Navy Lieutenant Paula Coughlin's accounts led to the re-investigation. Admiral Schachte sought proper adjudication. Photo courtesy U.S. Navy.

"I convinced the Chief of Naval Operations and others to have a consolidated convening authority to decide which cases should go to trial, or disposed, or dismissed. We had more than one hundred sailors and Marines who were implicated.

"I decided to recommend a vice-admiral who was then the Commander of Naval Surface Force Atlantic. Paul Reason was a USNA grad and the senior minority officer in the Navy, and he had a reputation for being independent and fair. He would be an excellent choice," Schachte pronounced.

There would be other authorities to convince on Capitol Hill.

"I was also asked to address the Women's Caucus on the Hill. The women's group included Senator Dianne Feinstein—then, a Congresswoman—as well as Congresswoman Pat Schroeder. Our meeting room was packed. There was a long table with me sitting at the head. It was a seemingly-hostile environment for a male authority figure in a male-caused crisis."

"I started off explaining the idea of a Consolidated Convening Authority as authorized under the UCMJ (Uniform Code of Military Justice). I also had a folder—a CV (curriculum vitae) at my side that included an 8x10 photo of Admiral Paul Reason. I felt that we needed his abilities," Schachte expressed.

"As soon as Congresswoman Schroeder saw the CV and photo of Admiral Reason, she passed the folder to Senator Feinstein. I was watching the passing of the folder to assess their reaction. That folder made the rounds, and the mood changed. The meeting went well. The caucus seemed settled that the plan of a consolidated convening authority and the insertion of Admiral Paul Reason was a step in the right direction," Schachte recalled.

"I then invited them, the Women's Caucus, and others to fly out for an overnight on a carrier off Norfolk. Oddly, when I wrapped the meeting up, some actually clapped before they caught themselves," Schachte recalled. "It was certainly not the time for clapping. We had a job to perform, and there was justice in the balance. But I felt I had gained their confidence to open the reinvestigation and get to the truth of all that had happened. The perpetrators would not escape justice. There was a chance for Lt. Coughlin and the other victims to see a fair and appropriate outcome."

"We all wanted this to be adjudicated properly, and Congress needed a pathway. I believe that my recommendation provided that," he added.

"When I back briefed at the Pentagon, Navy leadership had already heard about the meeting but not about my invite to a carrier. They didn't care too much for that suggestion, but it went down all right, and several Congressional staffers went out, as well. There were three officers with me, two military justice experts, and a captain from OLA (Office of Legislative Affairs). Captain Mike Bowman later retired as a three-star. He accompanied me to the Pentagon for the back-briefs," Schachte related.

"As a consequence of being forthright and reporting the facts—whether they were related to the Tailhook Scandal or the seemingly endless investigation related to the USS Iowa-- there would be fallout. It was a given, but there was an upside often overlooked. Getting to the truth was always the ultimate goal," Schachte conceded.

"I had been forewarned by many inside the Navy about the likely fallout. These were friends who saw the premature end of my career. There would be no chance of advancement after this high-profile set of trials began. There were too many personalities tied to too many others in positions of authority. The ugly would become even more ugly, as we uncovered facts and passed on criminal charges," Schachte recalled. "The deeper this went, the more I would be vilified for exposing it."

"Some of my friends who had advised me along the way suggested that there were possibly those in government, in the top brass, and even among the retired Navy brass that might have a problem with my directness. Despite the expected repercussions, my job was to get to the truth and to perform my duties accordingly. There were a small number of those that felt that I should have stopped short of those goals," Schachte noted. "That was never going to be the case."

"Post Tailhook, there was a departure of the responsible senior JAG officers and other officials implicated in the cover-up. Because of my leading role in the follow-up and corrective investigative actions, I became the subject of numerous 'hotline' calls placed in retribution anonymously.

"The 'hotline' was a system set up as a vehicle to report illegal activities in the services as a way to ferret out waste, fraud, and abuses in the military. Unfortunately, the system itself could be abused to tarnish the reputation of otherwise innocent individuals," Schachte detailed. "In a perfect world, the hotline information could be very helpful and advance much. But with the anonymity came a price. No one was responsible for what was portrayed in the hotline—factually or falsely—so hotline abuses were all too frequent. The hotline could be used as a weapon.

"If a person were a flag officer, or a civilian member of the SES (Senior Executive Service), that person's name would be placed on a 'tracker list' which is shared with senior members of that person's military department," Schachte further explained.

Though the hotline was well-intentioned, it did create a retributive and subversive side that initiated unwarranted, punitive investigations and reports.

"During my last year of active duty, my name was on the Navy tracker list. Finally, a new Navy Inspector General, a three-star vice admiral, took over those responsibilities in the normal rotation of his previous duties. Upon his arrival he was briefed on all pending cases. When he got to my name he decided to further investigate.

"Among other things he learned that some of my detractors had gained an ally in the press—specifically a reporter with a San Diego newspaper who included my name in some of his published articles. After a thorough review of all allegations that began with the hotline, the Navy Inspector General consulted with the DOD Inspector General. With his concurrence, he wrote a letter to the Secretary of the Navy.

"The letter noted that between January 1992 and January 1993 a series of anonymous hotline complaints and allegations had been made to both his office and the DOD Inspector General regarding me. The report listed some of them. He concluded that all were 'determined to be without basis or merit'. His final paragraph stated that he 'could not remember any naval officer who had undergone more intense scrutiny without the opportunity to confront a single accuser.' He added that I had 'been found faultless by thorough investigations' and that I 'had passed every test for integrity.' I was not aware of his report until I had received a copy of it a few days later, on August 9, 1993," Schachte stated. In fact, the Navy's Inspector general concluded his August 9, 1993 letter to the Secretary of the Navy stating "Bill Schachte has had a distinguished career and has served our nation and our Navy faithfully and well."

"There were those who had been impacted by the fallout that came from Tailhook. Looking back, there was no way I would survive my role there in, getting to the truth unscathed. It was my duty. Despite the expected negative impact on my career, I knew that I had to perform it with a blind eye to anything else but justice," Schachte concluded. "I did what I knew in my bones was right."

"On another level, NIS, which became popular on television later as NCIS, had some intriguing investigations. The 'C' was added to emplace the word 'Criminal.' So, 'Naval Investigative Service' became 'Naval

Criminal Investigative Service.' That additional letter happened after the Tailhook Scandal.

"You cannot imagine the number of criminal cases we were handling each year," Schachte stated. "It was difficult and intense work for our entire team."

"Near the end of my command at NIS, I had the occasion to correspond with the brilliant author Tom Clancy. My senior staff knew that we were friends and had asked me to contact him with the idea to infuse some of our stories and identity-protected agents in his books. I had previously met Tom Clancy at the Naval War College in Newport, Rhode Island.

"He was very gracious. He had been behind schedule with his publisher but was aware of what he called the 'hit jobs' done on us by the New York Times. He called me about the suggestion and apologized that he was too far behind the publisher's schedule to include citing our work at NIS. I asked him the name of the book he was working on. He answered, 'Clear and Present Danger.' He said he'd be very interested in putting NIS into a future novel."

Author Tom Clancy (1947-2013) became one of America's most popular novelists to incorporate the service of brilliant government officials into a genre dubbed "techno thrillers."[111] His fictional protagonist Jack Ryan worked for the CIA.[112] Among Clancy's bestsellers were *The Hunt for Red October*, *Patriot Games*, *Clear and Present Danger*, and *The Sum of All Fears*.[113] Schachte and Clancy enjoyed a mutually beneficial relationship over their respective careers.

Schachte's next assignment was the appointment to the post of Commander, Naval Legal Service Command. It was a natural progression the two-star admiral had earned. His reputation for fairness had been fully established.

William Schachte was named as Acting Judge Advocate General of the Navy 1992-1993. According to the USN regulations, the Judge Advocate General of the Navy, involves three key roles.[114] First the JAG serves as staff assistant to the Secretary of the Navy. He or she also commands the offices of the Judge Advocate General, or OJAG. Lastly, the role he or she serves is as Chief of the Judge Advocate General Corps.[115] Under Schachte, this group detailed over 1,100 officers serving as judge advocates, along with another small set of limited-law officers. The OJAG staff had over five hundred enlisted members (legalmen). Add in another four hundred civilian personnel.

A View of the White House with the Washington Monument in the background. Photo by Author.

By federal statute, the selection of a Judge Advocate General is from judge advocates of the Navy or Marine Corps who are members of the bar of a Federal court or the highest court of a State and who have had at least eight years of experience in legal duties as commissioned officers. The Judge Advocate General for many years had been appointed as a two-star rear admiral. In 2008, the National Defense Authorization Act changed the rank to three-star vice admiral (or lieutenant general for USMC).[116]
"When I saw that change in the appointment level, I had been retired for several years. I asked a few colleagues if it could be retroactive so

that I could get a promotion," Schachte smiled. "Having served, I am in agreement that the ranking JAG should meet a higher standard."

The Judge Advocate General is nominated for appointment by the President of the United States by recommendation of the Secretary of the Defense and/or the Secretary of the Navy. He or she must be confirmed by a majority vote of the U.S. Senate for a four-year term of office. However, historically, they serve for three years or less.[117]

Commanders, Naval Legal Service Command

Rear Admiral John Smith Jenkins	1980-1982
Rear Admiral James Joseph McHugh	1982-1984
Rear Admiral Thomas Edward Flynn	1984-1986
Rear Admiral Hugh Don Campbell	1986-1988
Rear Admiral Everett D. Stumbaugh	1988-1990
Rear Admiral William Leon Schachte, Jr.	**1990-1992**
Rear Admiral Harold E. Grant	1993-1994
Rear Admiral Carlson E. Legrand	1994-1997
Rear Admiral Donald J. Guter	1997-2000
Rear Admiral Michael Franklin Lohr	2000-2002
Rear Admiral James E. McPherson	2002-2004
Rear Admiral Bruce E. MacDonald	2004-2006
Rear Admiral James W. Houck	2006-2009
Vice Admiral Nanette DeRenzi	2009-2012
Vice Admiral James W. Crawford, III.	2012-2015
Rear Admiral John G. Hannink	2015-2018
Rear Admiral Darse E. Crandall, Jr.	2018-Incumbent

CHAPTER 17

Private Life in the Holy City

"After I retired from the Navy, I came back home to Charleston and Carmen, and I eventually moved into the home we bought in 1973. We had rented it, and at one time had four families living in our home. It is an 1884 Victorian style architecture in the historic section of the City," Schachte recounted.

The home was built in the Charleston tradition, with piazzas facing the prevailing southeasterly breezes. The common man's air-conditioning—high ceilings on both floors--are characteristic as they collect and dissipate the summer swelter. The corner lot borders Broad and Trapman streets.

"I started out working with the prestigious statewide law firm Nexsen Pruet in their Charleston office. My dear friend and former fraternity brother, Neil Robinson, serves the firm as the managing partner. Neil, originally from Columbia, became a highly-respected person in the Charleston community and wonderful friend, and I should add—a brilliant attorney. I enjoyed that time but felt I could better serve if I were in the D.C. area. I certainly didn't feel like moving my family back to D.C. David, our youngest, was about to start college and Billy had graduated from Clemson in 1989. I also started an interdenominational Bible Fellowship in Charleston," Schachte recalled. He had set up a busy schedule between two cities.

The Schachte Family in St. Thomas, USVI. L-R Billy, David, Carmen, and the retired Admiral. Photo courtesy of Schachte Family Archives.

"While working with clients at Nexsen Pruet, I had an offer to become a house counsel with a major DOD (Department of Defense) construction firm, Foster Wheeler Environmental Corporation. They sent me an offer which I, in turn, sent to my dear friend and colleague, Jim Ellis, who at the time had started his own law firm in Washington, D.C. Those offices were in the infamous Watergate Hotel building. Jim reviewed the contract offer for me and recommended that I sign it. Then he asked if I would like to be associated with his law firm. The firm's partners had discussed it, and they wanted to extend an offer to me. I accepted that. For the next thirteen years, I worked with that law firm. They later merged with Blank Rome—an international firm based in Philadelphia with other stateside offices. Blank Rome had an office in Hong Kong. I did work for the entire firm but primarily with their Watergate offices. My relationship that started with Foster Wheeler Environmental Corporation and their law firm was terrific.

"I served as a special counsel with Foster Wheeler and did more in the senior management arena and business development than legal work. During one of the senior management meetings offsite, I received a telephone call from the Dean of the Law School at Michigan State.

"My clients and I had just finished our morning session and were breaking for lunch. I was sitting next to the firm's president and CEO, Sam Box, who remains a respected and dear friend of mine. Sam couldn't help but overhear the conversation that I was having on this call.

"It turned out that the Dean had gotten my name from the Law of the Sea Institute in Honolulu, Hawaii. He was on the hook to provide a professor to teach a short survey course in international law and the Law of the Sea at the principal law school in Lithuania. The school is in the ancient city of Kaunus," Schachte remembered.

Kaunus is the second-largest city in Lithuania.[118] It was originally settled by the Romans at the confluence of the country's two largest rivers.[119]

"I was telling the gentleman on the phone that I really didn't have the available time and that I appreciated the offer. Sam Box asked me to hold the phone for a minute, and he and I spoke about what was being discussed. He encouraged me to accept, saying that I had already performed that month's required time under my retainer. I returned to the call and found that I could bring Carmen with me and that clinched the deal. I accepted the opportunity," Schachte stated. "I was off to the Baltics."

Vytautas the Great Bridge crosses the Neman river into Kaunas, Lithuania.

"Carmen and I went to Lithuania, and it turned out to be a grand experience. We arrived in Lithuania about a week before Easter. When we got there, after several flights, it was snowing, and it remained very cold the whole time we were there. At one point, the dean of the school asked me if I could truncate my course. Instead of making it two weeks, he asked if I could teach everything in one week. I was teaching in an auditorium of the senior students. The only adjustment I had was to speak slowly. They all understood English and also knew Russian and of course, Lithuanian.

"I told them that I could undoubtedly teach it in one week instead of two, but I would have to extend an hour's teaching in the evenings, and one hour in each class. The plan worked, and we got the entire course completed in that one long week.

"When I told Carmen about the change of plans and the shortened course period, she was excited. She said, 'Great, we will travel.' She was happy to gain the experience and for the two of us to spend time abroad," Schachte warmly reflected. "She liked having the extra free time."

Traveling in the northern European climate before the thaw of the wintertime was concerning, but not enough to cause the cancellation of plans.

"I called a friend of mine in Berlin, and he advised that we not go to Berlin. The Iraq War was just starting and the local people there were not too happy with us Americans. So, we decided instead to go to Poland. We were trying to determine how best to get to Poland. We were told not to take planes because they were extraordinarily expensive and not that safe. We were also advised not to go by train because they hadn't been worked on since the Germans were in control of the country. We found that the buses were all new and double-deckers. I had the hotel concierge drive Carmen and me to the bus station where we bought a round trip ticket to Warsaw.

"Carmen and I left from the hotel to the bus station the next morning for our 8 a.m. departure. We saw the fleet of new and impressive double-decker busses except one. Of course, that was our bus. It was an old gray bus. I went aboard, because it was an eight-hour trip, to check out to make sure they had restroom facilities. There was a big strap over the restroom door. I found a student who had a lot of books and was talking with people in French and German. I asked him if he knew English, and he responded,

'Yes.' I asked him to please ask the bus driver if the toilet worked. So, he went over, and I saw him talking to the bus driver in Lithuanian. They both started to laugh, and he came back and said it works but only at stops.

I asked in astonishment, 'Only at stops?'

"The driver replied, 'Yes, we make a lot of stops, and that is when people can go to the bathroom.'"

"So, I told Carmen, 'I don't know if I want to do this.'"

"She said, 'No, we are going to do it. I've made sandwiches, and I have some wine, and we will have a grand time.' Carmen convinced me."

The adventure was on.

"We loaded into this old rickety bus. There were only about ten of us. The bus capacity was fifty. Off we went. It was a gear shift bus. It took the heating system almost an hour to warm the bus up. As I noticed, I turned to Carmen, and I said, 'Look, this guy knows all the backroads to get to the main highway between the capital of Lithuania, Vilnius, and Warsaw. As it turned out, all of those one-car bridges we encountered were on the main highway. It was approaching the springtime planting season. The only farmers we saw were spreading seed usually from the back of a wagon pulled by oxen. We didn't see any mechanized machinery until we were about ten miles outside of Warsaw. It was as if they were living in a prior century. We got to Warsaw. It was an adventurous trip. We decided the next day to go to Krakow. We took the train. Polish trains were really good. Then we took the bus back to Vilnius. This time we boarded a new double-decker bus. It stopped at several very nice places along the way. We were happy not to be on that old gray gear-shift bus. That old bus to Warsaw was a nightmare, but Carmen and her picnic lunches made it an adventure."

"I continued my career with Foster Wheeler Environmental which had been bought out by Tetra Tech and Blank Rome. I had turned seventy-four after working with both firms for thirteen years after my Navy retirement. I again returned to Charleston and began more volunteer work than anything else—which I enjoy. Carmen and I have always felt that we should all find the time and energy to give back.

"It can make a difference," the admiral related. "Besides, volunteer work keeps you young and engaged."

"Looking back, when I worked my way through law school, my last assignment was as the student assistant to the Dean of the Law School—Dean Bob Foster. After I retired and started practicing law in Charleston, I went up to the law school to visit with some of my previous professors. I was asked if I would be interested in teaching a course on International Law. It was appealing to me to get back to law school just to see the students and try to give back. I had a fair amount of experiences in actually practicing international law at the Pentagon and with the JAG Corps. I accepted the USC Law School request. I taught over two separate semesters at the law school. I enjoyed that mainly because Carmen would ride up with me the hour and a half to Columbia. I would teach my class, and she would visit my sister who was living in the area. We would often visit Fort Jackson, or we would go out and enjoy lunch together.

"We would typically stop at the assisted living facility in Summerville, South Carolina, where my Aunt Jree was living at the time and have supper with her. I enjoyed teaching the students at the School of Law but not to the extent that I would teach full time. I was encouraged because I had received outstanding ratings from my students," Schachte said. "It is certainly a privilege to help influence and instruct young minds."

"Perhaps some of them had never considered a scenario where an admiral would teach them law. I felt anything but out of place there. It was a solid and memorable experience," Schachte said. "I'm glad I accepted the request."

The admiral had become involved in the areas that both challenged and comforted his persona. He assisted with other social and community endeavors—most notably being drafted by his cousin, Joe Riley, to take a lead role in his political campaign. In 1994, Riley ran for governor of the State of South Carolina as the Democratic Party primary opponent to eventual nominee Nick Theodore. Theodore lost to the Republican candidate, David Beasley.[120]

Beyond politics, Schachte sought and performed substantial charitable volunteer and parish duties in the Charleston community. The admiral attended many civic events while remaining vigilant in his faith as a daily attendee at the noonday Mass at the Cathedral of St. John the Baptist.

"One would suspect that, in retirement, there would be a respite. I filled my schedule often enough to keep both Carmen and me as busy as I was in the Navy. In Charleston, that's easy to do. The old city has a very active community," Schachte explained. "Besides, I had some catching up to do with many childhood friends."

After 136 years, the H.L. Hunley was recovered and a restoration process ensued. Schachte was appointed as RDA Chairman with plans to move the submarine and artifacts to a museum. Photo courtesy of Charleston RDA.

Schachte serves as the Chairman of the Redevelopment Authority (RDA) charged with the responsibility of building a permanent home for *CSS Hunley*. The H.L. Hunley submarine was raised from the seabed off Charleston's coast in 2000. It has been meticulously preserved. The Hunley made maritime history, when, on February 12, 1864, it attacked and sunk the *USS Housatonic* in Charleston harbor. It was the first sinking of an enemy vessel by a submarine in the history of warfare. The novelty of the 136-year period between its wartime action and recovery brought the world press to Charleston. After nearly twenty years of preservation work, the Hunley and as many as 10,000 maritime artifacts are planned to be placed into a state-of-the-art maritime museum at Patriots Point. The facility will be located just across the harbor from where the incident occurred. Admiral Schachte's role in leading that effort has drawn the deserved praise of the community.

"Many will look at the Hunley Museum project in different ways. I see it as the preservation of a new technology—akin to finding the Wright Brothers first airplane. The Hunley changed the world—not as many infer, on a military basis—but for scientific and exploration reasons. There are even recreational submersibles all over. If not for that technology and the later iterations, we would not have key knowledge of our planet," Schachte offered. "The new Hunley Museum will teach later generations about the wonders of the sea."

Schachte has been most attentive to his lifelong desire to see new and interesting places with his wife and favorite companion, Carmen. They plan trips, which he cites as "adventures." His 2019 trip to the Inside Passage of Alaska by cruise was accompanied by friends from his alma mater, Clemson University.

Billy and Carmen Schachte discovering the glaciers from a cruise ship in Alaska, 2019. Photo courtesy Schachte family archives.

"Carmen and I love to get out and spend time with family and friends whenever we have a chance. The world offers many interesting places to visit, and we enjoy these experiences immensely," Schachte offered. "The one thing we don't seem to do is 'nothing.' We like going to places and getting involved. Life is short. Enjoy it.

That's why God put us here—to make a difference and to find our spiritual center within His providence."

CHAPTER 18
Coming Around Again

The admiral could have retired peacefully knowing that he spent his career in service to his faith, his family, and his country. He had fought in Vietnam. He had faced down the Soviets resolutely within his field of expertise—international maritime law. He had commanded a "fleet" of 1,100 naval lawyers in his role at the head of Naval Legal Service Command. He had adjudicated what had become a major story of scandal known as "Tailhook." He was chosen because of his demonstrated abilities, pertinent knowledge, and unquestioned commitment to truth and honesty.

It would have been a more comfortable post-naval career to continue his hobbies and passions that were forestalled by his absolute dedication to duty.

He and Carmen had bought an old Charleston home in 1973—knowing they would eventually return to their family and friends they enjoyed. The house had to be repaired and remodeled. Schachte's vast law experience and military insight qualified him as a valuable asset, especially to larger law firms. He found a great fit with Nexsen Pruet, a firm with nearly 200 lawyers in eight cities across the Carolinas. He was home again.

But something happened in 2004.

"On the night that John Kerry was nominated by the Democratic National Convention to be the standard-bearer for the Democratic Party for the 2004 Presidential Election, Carmen and I were driving back to Charleston. We were returning from a funeral at Arlington National Cemetery for an admiral friend of ours. We picked up the Democratic National Convention on PBS and were able to follow it on PBS stations.

I was feeling almost ill listening to all that stuff about someone whom I knew quite a lot, perhaps too much. Personally, I couldn't believe that the American public could be so totally fooled," Schachte began.

"When the Democratic Convention came to the conclusive nomination, Senator John Kerry stood in front of everyone and saluted and said he was reporting for duty. I really thought I was going to vomit. So, as the Latin expression goes, '*Alea iacta est*'[121]—the die was cast. All of the Swift Boat guys eventually got together who had served with Lieutenant (junior grade) Kerry in Vietnam. They were certainly not supporting him.

"Later the Swift Boaters had also been joined by some Prisoners of War who had joined the *Swift Boat Veterans for Truth* because some of them had been tortured more extensively for refusing to acknowledge as truth the lies that Kerry told to the Senate Foreign Relations Committee under oath."

Schachte placed the moment in perspective.

"After Kerry's book [*Tour of Duty: John Kerry and the Vietnam War (2004)*] was published, everyone had an opportunity to review his version of what happened in Vietnam. It was a load of malarkey. His first Purple Heart was the one that I was involved in—and I knew that it was a fake. He shot too low, albeit accidentally, while we were running an ambush in a 15-foot skimmer to which he referred to as a Boston Whaler in his book. The plan was what I had devised, to draw fire from the enemy. I had come up with it—trying to be proactive in going against infiltration of arms and NVA into our operating areas," Schachte recalled.

The details of Kerry's erstwhile "Purple Heart One" were given in a 2012 book, *Sunsets Over Charleston*. The admiral placed the parameters.

"*It was in Vietnam that Schachte devised a way to entice the Viet Cong into impromptu firefights that were planned traps. It was part of the use of 'SWIFT Boats' and Navy skimmers. A SWIFT boat is an acronym for a 'Shallow Water Inshore Fast Tactical' watercraft.*[122] *Schachte's plan was well thought out.*

"*Essentially, I would take two volunteers out on a skimmer towed by a SWIFT Boat and then troll alone near a shoreline. I'd have an enlisted man on the motor and another junior officer on one of the two weapons. We also carried an M69 grenade launcher and illuminator flares. I insisted on volunteers due to the danger of the mission. We'd leave the SWIFT Boat after midnight with a FAC aircraft on alert. (FAC, or 'forward air control' naval planes were used as needed to support such missions.) We were trying to lure fire from the Viet Cong. I'd look for enemy movement or noise of any kind. If we saw something, we'd open up with our weapons (an M-60 machine gun and an M-16 mounted with a starlight into the area trying to draw the return fire. If firepower was returned, we'd get out quickly calling in the positions for both Naval artillery and tree-top air support, if available."* Schachte explained. *"The plan had worked a few times. But I felt like since it was my idea, I needed to be the first volunteer for each mission."*

On the night of December 2, 1968, LT Schachte took a raw volunteer with him on the exercise. That volunteer was LTJG (Lieutenant Junior Grade) John Kerry. At about 3:00 a.m., as he described it, Schachte thought he saw movement, and he fired a handheld illumination flare. He immediately fired in the direction of the movement, as did Kerry. But Kerry's gun jammed. Kerry then manned the grenade launcher and fired off the first round. A piece of Shrapnel from the "blow back" range of the grenade nicked his upper arm. No return fire was detected. Seeing nothing, Schachte ordered a ceasefire. He then returned to the SWIFT boat that was standing by. Once there, a decision was made to not file the mandatory 'after action' report since no enemy was encountered. Schachte had admonished Kerry for firing the M69 grenade launcher too closely as shrapnel could have easily taken out an eye.

Schachte went to bed upon returning to Cam Ranh Bay, planning on a late wake-up from his post-sunrise return.

"I was awakened with a message from the skipper, Commander Grant Hibbard. He wanted me in his office immediately," Schachte recounted. "I was startled and wondering what was up. When I got there, John Kerry was already there. He had requested a Purple Heart! Commander Hibbard asked about my report. I had briefed him earlier that there was no enemy fire. When I repeated to him there was no enemy return fire, he became incensed at Kerry. In Naval language laced with a few choice words, he told Kerry 'to get out of his office.'"

"Kerry was transferred out within about two weeks. I had not heard from him again until he had become a senator. We saw each other under the Capitol waiting on a senate subway. He remembered that my call sign that night was 'Batman.' He said we should get together for lunch, but that never happened. I thought I'd heard the last of Kerry and that 'SWIFT Boat' incident until he ran for president in 2004. That's when his book came out titled <u>Tour of Duty</u>. In it, it was pointed out to me by someone else, that he detailed his Purple Heart awards including one he did eventually receive somehow from the incident I described in 1968. The doctor that attended him said it was a scratch that he applied a Band-Aid and ointment to. I gave no report because there was no enemy confrontation – one of the conditions necessary for both a written report and an award of a Purple Heart. Commander Grant Hibbard threw Kerry out of his office for requesting a Purple Heart. So, how did he politically arrange this self-inflicted scratch into an actual Purple Heart?"

When the race between Democratic nominee John Kerry and incumbent President George W. Bush heated up, these claims again came to the forefront. A second Vietnam Conflict Purple Heart was characterized as also self-inflicted. It stemmed from Kerry blowing up an absconded container of rice and injuring his buttocks in the process. This was attested to have happened by another SWIFT boat officer. In time, an organization was formed to challenge the Kerry claims. They called themselves the 'SWIFT Boat Veterans for Truth.'

Being somewhat apolitical, Schachte did not join.

Massachusetts Senator John Kerry in 2012. Kerry served in Vietnam under Schachte's command. Photo by Author.

In 2004, he (Schachte) had already contributed $1,000 to the Bush campaign.

"My donation was not so much because I liked George Bush, but because I knew the Kerry character," Schachte explained.

Yet Schachte previously went on record as voting for Democrat Bill Clinton in his first election prior to Bush's stint in the White House. The pundits came out of the woodwork. The Dems looked for Schachte motives. They even made up a few. The Republicans asked for interviews. Schachte wisely stayed the course, not looking for the avalanche of media attention. He declined interviews from popular television network journalist Sean Hannity, along with requests from other networks. He deflected endless criticism from the left. In time, he agreed to an on-camera interview with NBC's Lisa Meyers (printed in its entirety below). The hour and a half interview took place on August 24th, 2004, in plenty of time for the Kerry camp to try and refute the report prior to the November election. In it, Meyers asked in every conceivable way—multiple times—if Admiral Schachte was calling Senator John Kerry a liar. Schachte fell short of the obvious by referring directly to the chronology and reporting of the incident in question so that the listener could draw their own conclusions. Had Schachte, who had stayed on the sidelines, not come forward to tell the facts, many believe John Kerry may have beaten Bush in 2004. To this day, the political left holds Schachte accountable for the loss of the White House. A more prudent view would be that John Kerry brought it on himself.

It bears emphasis that there was no enemy combatant there that night and that the self-inflicted Kerry wound was mostly superficial. It was a small band-aid matter.

The admiral elaborated on the subject of coming forward to refute a high-profile presidential candidate.

"Part of why I felt so uneasy was because I knew myself too well. I knew the truth about that very questionable and unearned Purple Heart. From my schoolyard days at Sacred Heart School to today, I have always felt that what mattered above everything else was truth. I knew that my fellow veterans felt exactly as I did without talking to any of them.

"The lawyer side of me told me that I should stand down," Schachte stated. "But I couldn't live the rest of my life knowing that I knew the lie and did nothing. And I knew that Kerry, the Democratic machine, and even the slanted press would come after me—guns blazing. Carmen knew it, too. But even she knew that I had to stand up and that our lives would change dramatically."

The lawyer side of Schachte achieved a small victory. He would not join any political group. He had a history of donating across party lines—but never to a significant enough contribution to be considered an insider or a political operative. His highest lifetime contributions were limited to $1,000, and he sent then to both Democrats and Republicans.

"I sent donations to Fritz Hollings, Bill Clinton, Lindsey Graham, and George Bush. It was never enough to be noticed, and I remain basically apolitical," Schachte added.

"I was not with the new group of Swift Boat guys at the time. They got together and rented the National Press Club in Washington, D.C. Each man there got up and read his statement about what had happened. These statements were actually sworn depositions of the individuals who were told to go the local courthouse and swear out an affidavit. My incident was covered by two such people—my Division Commander, Grant Hibbard and Dr. Lewis Letson. Dr. Letson was the physician who took a minute curlycue shard out of Kerry's arm with tweezers and placed a band-aid on it after applying ointment. So, I began to think that the incident was well-documented—saving me what I knew would be the vitriol of public politics," Schachte stated.

"Commander Hibbard's report contained what I told him after that mission that John Kerry had accidentally injured himself. I reprimanded Kerry about the danger of shooting an M79 under such circumstances. There was some minor blame on me for letting Kerry go on that mission because he was a rookie and had never been in a firefight. A firefight is an experience unlike anything one can imagine. I accepted as just the criticism of my choice to allow him, a rookie, to come with me," Schachte reflected.

He further explained the reason he had to come forward.

"When John O'Neil's book, *Unfit for Command*, was published in the same year (2004), I was cited in that book concerning Kerry's first fake purple heart. The press immediately picked up on that item in the book and began trying to contact me. This drumbeat went on for quite a while. I knew it was coming and felt that I needed to be prepared to do as I had always done. Tell the facts. John O'Neill had been a stand-up guy, and it could be said that his well-researched book was really the downfall of John Kerry as a presidential candidate. I just became the next media target because I supported John O'Neill and the outstanding exposé, he wrote to save this country from John Kerry," Schachte stated.

"There was a protocol I needed to follow, given my profession. I told my principal client and my law firm that I was hoping not to get involved in that event, knowing that there were two people, our division commander and the doctor, who had covered my part of it. I explained to them that those facts did not satisfy the mainstream media, and I knew where it was going."

Things heated up.

"The media frenzy had begun. The enraged Democratic operatives began calling me a liar on national television. They quoted me from John O'Neill's book. The first to decide that I was a liar without ever speaking to me was Chris Matthews on his show *Hardball*. That was then picked up by Lanny Davis and all the Democratic apologists who were supporting the Kerry ticket.

"I had talked to my principal client in the law firm and told him that I could not remain silent under such circumstances. It was not right for the author of the book to be defending me. I needed to be defending myself because I was there, and I knew what the truth was—and the incident as stated in *Unfit for Command* was accurate," Schachte stated.

Schachte viewing the Vietnam coast in 1968. It was Vietnam all over again. The career naval officer recalled the truth vividly. Photo from Schachte family archives.

"My main client and my law firm were fully supportive of me. Everything in the O'Neill book is completely accurate other than our call signs of that evening. My skiff command call sign was 'Batman' and the Swift Boats' officer standing by had the call sign 'Robin.' With an enlisted motor operator and Kerry, three was a crowd for that small shallow skiff.

"My memory of that night was vivid because of the outlandish request Kerry made after we returned. He had put in for a Purple Heart without receiving enemy fire."

Schachte intimated that had John Kerry not filed the Purple Heart report to Captain Grant Hibbard, he would likely have forgotten that night.

There was an attorney-client-law firm process to follow before the admiral could forward his full witness version of the Kerry incident.

"I agreed to go public after I got clearance from my client and the firm. I didn't want to grandstand on the matter. It was never my way. Truly, I just wanted to get it off my conscience by telling the truth. When you think about it, I was the third confirmation of the same story with Skip Hibbard and Dr. Letson. Maybe they were hoping I would refute it," Schachte said. "Everybody wanted to hear it from me because I was there and witnessed the supposed enemy action—a firefight that never was."

"I agreed to one television interview and I was hoping to get one nationally syndicated columnist to discuss my statement. That happened, and I turned down a number of conservative leaning outlets and decided to go with NBC," Schachte explained.

All of the major networks and radio hosts had called constantly to get the interview. The admiral knew that whatever he said would be hoisted by one group and buried by the other. He chose the NBC venue because he felt that, though they had demonstrated a mostly left-leaning sentiment, they would allow him to speak and get the truth out. It was the after-truth grilling that concerned him. It was not—and is not—unusual for large media giants to posture the truth in hurricane winds to twist it into something unrecognizable. He did not want to see a headline the next day that quoted one dramatic line out of the context of the entire interview.

He recalled the beginnings.

"The reporter, Lisa Myers, had really been after me and somehow obtained my unlisted cell phone number and the numbers of my home phone and my beach house number. My law firm leadership told me that they wanted me to talk with a PR firm that they used to help people with the press—knowing that I would be really 'jumping the shark' when I went public on this. It was some ten weeks before a presidential election. My law firm was comprised of all sectors of the political spectrum and yet they were behind me one hundred percent. I met with the PR folks and with their help, I told them that I wanted to go with NBC, as I felt comfortable that Ms. Myers would put both sides out—though the consensus was that the network would try and undermine my story somehow."

Schachte continued the rollout of the events.

"As far as a column was concerned, Robert Novak contacted me and asked to speak with me. I told him what had happened that night, and he readily agreed to do a nationally-syndicated column on the situation which he did.

"I was then contacted by the PR folks helping me. I was told I would have a conference call with Lisa Myers on a Friday afternoon at 3:00 p.m. I took the call, of course. My media person was on the phone to help from Washington. Lisa Myers was joined by two producers in New York City and two producers in Washington on that same conference call. She started out by explaining that they could not use anything that I had not agreed to allow. She stated that the conference conversation would be off the record unless I agreed to let them utilize what I was saying. She then went on to tell me that they were going to put this on the air in a couple of months. We had plenty of time before the election, and they were in no hurry.

"Myers then began with, 'Admiral I understand you know John Kerry.' I said, 'Yes ma'am, let me tell you the story.' I then proceeded to talk straight for about 35 minutes.

"When I finished, there was dead silence on the phone, and the next voice was Lisa Myers who asked, 'Can you get to Washington in a couple of days? We want to get this out very quickly.' I agreed to go to Washington and had the interview with her. But before I did this, I let some of my friends know—those whom I had told I was hoping to stay completely on the sidelines given that the story had already been told in the John O'Neill book. All three witnesses were cited in the book, so I felt that the sheer concordance bore the facts out.

"But the press was fully engaged by then," Schachte noted.

"They were hungry. I think even my friends knew that I couldn't let the Kerry incident pass as 'the valor that never was.' It was going to get rough," Schachte conceded.

Author John O'Neill served in the United States Navy from 1967 to 1971. The U.S. Naval Academy graduate spent nearly three years of his service in Vietnam including the command of John Kerry's former Swift Boat. It was the same PCF4 Swift Boat that Kerry once commanded in Coastal Division 11. O'Neill was outraged by Kerry's nefarious claims of valor in Vietnam. He researched them meticulously and challenged Kerry on the facts. They had earlier faced each other in a debate on the *Dick Cavett Show* in 1971 when Kerry was an outspoken anti-war protestor. Kerry's organization, "Veterans Against the Vietnam War" was countermanded by O'Neill's representation of the organization, "Vietnam Veterans for a Just Peace."

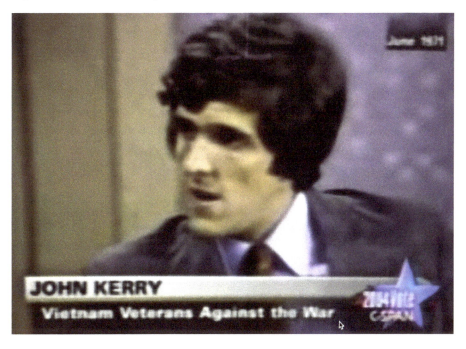

Activist John Kerry appeared in a debate forum on the Dick Cavett Show with former Swift Boat commander John O'Neill in 1971. Kerry lost his bid for a contested US House seat the next year and left politics for a decade. Photo courtesy of YouTube.

"Admiral Schachte is a hero to me," O'Neill stated. "He had nothing to gain and everything to lose when he decided to stand up and tell the truth. He was up for a judgeship he would never get after his brave counterclaim to the first Kerry Purple Heart, a fake. He likely lost clients in his firm's law practice. There is no way of knowing how much income he may have lost. And he lost many of his friends who were so wrapped up in politics that they didn't want to know the truth."

"Had Billy Schachte not stood up, there was much more at stake. The second and third Kerry Purple Heart claims were vehemently contested by those who were there. Those that served with Kerry, I found, had no use for him. They saw the obvious narcissism. And then he went on to betray their service, and the service of so many that died honorably in Vietnam. But the media was ready to give Kerry a pass. With Grant 'Skip' Hibbard's story hanging in the balance, only Billy Schachte's first-hand account mattered. The media could not pass on that," O'Neill detailed.

He clarified the timing that changed the 2004 presidential election.

"When I wrote my book, *Unfit for Command*, the columnist Robert Novak made it clear to me that he would get behind me with Schachte's testimony to support the false Kerry 'Purple Heart One.' But without Schachte's story, he would pass. Novak knew that Schachte's story would change everything. Novak determined that Schachte had too much to lose to come forward. But the admiral's patriotism, honor and selflessness superseded all else."

Indeed, O'Neill was right. Once word got out that the admiral was going on national television to speak the truth, he found that some didn't want the truth. It didn't suit their agenda.

Schachte explained.

"Somewhat to my surprise, I starting to receive calls from people who I thought were dear friends of mine who were also Democrats. I was being told things like, 'Bill, you don't have any idea what you are getting into—there are millions of dollars involved in this. If you get into the middle of it, you will have the biggest target on your back of anyone involved, and it will destroy your health. It could ruin your family and will have long-lasting adverse consequences to your career and your life.'

"I continued to get calls such as that—particularly from one person whom I had previously considered to be a dear friend who was very much a Democrat first—I learned. My last call from this individual was while I was in D.C. I was in the dressing room ready to go into the studio to be interviewed by Lisa Myers. I didn't take the call. It was on my voice mail. I let my media person in Washington listen to it. She asked to borrow my phone, so she could transcribe what was said. It wasn't nice.

Author John O'Neill's experiences were even worse. There were anonymous threats; loud shots fired into a phone call receiver and continuous other startling harassments. People even came to picket his daughter's wedding.

O'Neill, who clerked for Supreme Court Justice William Rehnquist, has practiced law for more than three decades in the Houston area.

"When you inject your sense of honor and justice into the political arena by doing the right thing despite the consequences, you become a target. Schachte saw these tactics first-hand. They try to censor you, to vilify you, to intimidate you, and even to intimidate your family. It's a sad comment on the state of our country's political divide," O'Neill stated. "Telling the truth comes with tremendous upheaval."

Schachte's experiences continued to decline after he came forward, as well. The calls from former friends enraged by the likely political consequences continued. Carmen Schachte answered many of the calls at home. She was cordial to all but firm. Most wanted him to stand down from the scheduled Lisa Myers interview on national television.

Schachte was not going to withdraw from what he had witnessed thirty-six years earlier. He felt that he could not betray the Vietnam veterans, the U.S. Navy, his country, and importantly, all that he believed in for his entire life. He could not walk away from truth.

"I went on set and sat down with Lisa Myers for over an hour. [See transcription in the following chapter.] I had a long conversation prior to that time with Robert Novak. I was on national television one week from the date of my telephone interview. Robert Novak's nationally syndicated column appeared in papers that Friday morning, and that Friday evening I was on NBC news and subsequent programs sponsored by MSNBC.

There was almost immediate fallout. He explained the repercussions.

"I had nothing to hide, but you should know that they'll make up something. The interview was followed by an accusation of the Kerry campaign that I 'changed by story' in order to get a $50 million-dollar grant for a client in Philadelphia. I had no idea of this grant. My law firm was aware of one, but I had done other work for the client previously and they always listed attorneys involved with people. So, some overzealous person did opposition research and concluded that I done something in return for this grant. Of course, it was diversion and was totally false. This was supposed to be concerning the shipyard in Philadelphia, a client who had developed a fast ship technology. The *Washington Post* printed a story about this accusation on the front page of their business section. That false charge, of course, was used by the Kerry campaign and likely sent to every campaign office in the Kerry organization. Almost immediately, an investigative reporter issued a story that the *Post* article was not accurate. Then the *Philadelphia Daily Enquirer* did a story the next day with the same conclusion that there was no basis for this accusation.

"I felt good about it until I got to the last sentence in that article which said, 'but nobody knows why the Admiral changed his story.' That was astounding because I had never even told my story before, so I had not changed anything. It's a political misdirection play. They say that a story was changed, but they never cite the first story. The bottom line is that you can't win in a situation like that," Schachte explained. "They have no rules."

The admiral was concerned about Carmen and his home life. It was also compelling to all that the Kerry camp had seemingly endless funding. Kerry, whose wife is the Heinz Foods heiress, was personally able to adapt to anything financially. He never heard from Kerry, and with all of his personal fortune, Kerry never threatened a lawsuit.

That obvious inaction by Kerry speaks to the credibility of Schachte versus Kerry.

"The phones in our home, our beach house, my cell phone, and all communications remained very active. That matter of the $50 million-dollar grant was also on television on a Saturday afternoon—just after the Friday evening that I was on television. They must've decided to use it in advance because it sounded good enough to deflect the Vietnam story.

They likely knew it wasn't true, but it could cast doubt on my character," Schachte explained.

He was knee-deep in a political assassination morass. Campaigns have full crisis management staffs used to deflect the negatives by casting doubt upon the sources. It's an art form promulgated upon the American voters from nearly every high-profile campaign.

"The story from the Philadelphia newspaper ran on Monday. There was another on Tuesday. That Tuesday afternoon, Carmen asked how many 'Frequent Flyer' miles I had saved. Since I had been dealing with clients on the West Coast, I had quite a few. She said, 'Good. Pack your clothes because we are going to take a trip. We're going to Scotland and maybe Ireland.' So, we did that. We went to Scotland and across the Irish Sea and spent time in Dublin. We traveled for about two weeks, and it felt very nice to be away from the endless political focus. Carmen insisted that I employ a news blackout. The only television I could watch was weather reports about the current weather conditions where we were. Other than that, it was a welcomed news blackout.

"My dear wife sure knows how to take care of me. We eventually returned home, and the election was held. Kerry lost to George W. Bush in a close vote."

Carmen and Bill Schachte were glad it was over. They could get back to their normal pace of life.

*Swift Boats patrolling the Vietnam coast.
Photo Courtesy Schachte Family Archives.*

The incumbent president George Bush won the electoral college vote 286-251.[123] He won the popular vote 51% to 48 %.[124] Kerry had a fragile lead of three percentage points in the polls prior to the Schachte interview on NBC.[125] Many of the political pundits from both parties conceded that the Swift Boat Veterans for Truth group and Admiral Schachte had made a significant enough difference. They likely changed the 2004 election results. John O'Neill's well-researched book, "Unfit for Command," was the catalyst.

Ohio, Iowa, and Florida were battleground states that the Kerry camp could not command. There were too many retired veterans in Florida who saw Kerry differently.

"Ironically, what I considered to be an unfortunate incident—that is— someone in the skiff could have gotten seriously injured by that grenade that Kerry launched too low. That comment turned out to be true. John

Kerry was "blown up" by that grenade launcher mishap. But the grenade took thirty-six years to explode. The truth prevailed.

"As insignificant as it was at the time, it all came back to the truth. He had three Purple Hearts recorded from his short Vietnam service. No one seems to know how he qualified for any of them. There were two other ones that were similarly undeserved—as testified to by those at the scene," Schachte retold. "At the very least, he tried to take advantage of his situation by padding his Vietnam résumé. But the dishonesty took away his lifelong ambition."

"Several years later a dear friend of mine met Kerry at some function in the Senate—a reception of some kind. Perhaps Kerry didn't know that we were good friends. This fellow was a retired Navy Captain helicopter pilot, not a JAG guy, and told Kerry that he knew me. He asked Kerry, 'So, what happened?' He told me that Kerry answered, 'I don't know what happened, Senator Hollings' people were supposed to take care of him.' I guess things were set to keep me from saying anything. I am not aware of a plan to shut me up that Senator Hollings was behind back then. In fact, I had contributed regularly to Senator Hollings' campaigns!"

Senator Ernest F. "Fritz" Hollings (1922-2019) served thirty-eight years in the United States Senate from South Carolina, and the admiral's mother made ceramics with the senator's mother. He was a lifelong Democrat and a friend of Admiral Schachte's.

The Lisa Myers interview commanded a discerning audience. Many were undecided voters. They had more than ten weeks to settle upon who was telling the truth—the retired admiral or the senator-candidate. Not looking for the attention, the admiral, nonetheless, felt compelled to set the record straight. In doing so, he may have changed history.

CHAPTER 19
Reprint: The Interview that Changed an Election

August 24, 2004 was only seventy-seven days prior to the competitive and close presidential election between the incumbent Republican George H. W. Bush and the Massachusetts Democrat John Kerry. When Admiral Schachte agreed to the interview, he knew it could have consequential impact upon the heated contest. Though it was not his intention to draw the spotlight of the national press and the endless talk show scrutiny, it was his duty to set so erroneous a record straight. His conviction for truth overcame his reticence to enter the fray.

Lisa Myers was a senior investigative reporter for NBC Nightly News. Myers was from Joplin, Missouri and graduated from the famed journalism school at the University of Missouri in Columbia. She had been with NBC for twenty-three years at the time of the interview and retired ten years later. She had a distinguished career to include awards in her field—an Emmy (2004) highlighted a handful of others.[126]

The following interview is a word-for-word reprint, courtesy of NBCNews.com. There are no corrections made herein. It is reprinted in its original form.

NBC's Lisa Myers conducted the following interview with Rear Adm. William L. Schachte (USN Ret.) in Washington, D.C. on Aug. 24, 2004. Portions have been edited for clarity.

Myers: When did you first meet John Kerry?

Adm. William Schachte (U.S. Navy, ret.): In Vietnam in 1968. I was – like everyone, by the way, serving on small boats in combat in Vietnam – I was a volunteer. When John reported aboard, I was then the lieutenant and the senior, second in command officer of Coastal Division 14. I was also the operations officer, and John reported sometime in mid-November – as an officer in charge under training. And that's the first time I met him.

Myers: And so, you were his superior?

Schachte: Yeah, I was one of his superiors, yes.

Myers: And how long did you serve with Senator Kerry?

Schachte: Until he left our area; I believe it was the 4th of December [1968] or so.

Myers: So, for a period of roughly how long?

Schachte: Well, a couple of weeks. Several weeks. But he was out on patrol and I was with him one night in particular – in the skimmer [*Note: Schachte claims the date of that night was 12/02/68, the same date listed in military records for the incident that earned Kerry his first Purple Heart; "skimmer" is a type of small water craft used by U.S. forces in Vietnam*]. Which was the subject of that first matter concerning his Purple Heart…

I had been a patrolling officer and when I became the operations officer and the number two in command, it was subsequent to the bombing halt announced by President Johnson. We got orders to turn up the heat, try to be more aggressive, do things differently. And I conceived an operation – it became known as 'skimmer ops.' Very simple operation – we had a 15-foot Boston whaler. We would send that boat into 'hot' areas… The operation was very simple. The boat was to go into these areas, and, by the way, I must mention that these areas were all non-population areas, not near any villages or anything else. We knew if anybody or anyone were around, they were enemy. We would go in, draw fire and get out immediately. Let others – swift boats standing off or maybe air support come in and take care of the enemy forces… [*"swift boat" was the common name for Patrol Craft Fast vessels (PCFs) used by the U.S. Navy in Vietnam*]

Myers: So, you were basically trying to smoke out the enemy?

Schachte: Yes. Bait 'em, if you will. We had these boats. We had an M-60 machine gun forward, an M-16 mounted with a starlight scope. On a hazy night, a badly overcast night, we had a M-14 mounted with an infra-red. M-79 grenade launcher – those were single-launch launchers in those days. Flares…an FM radio. And we, in addition to our combat gear – helmets, flak-jackets and what-not – we had .38-caliber pistols. I usually carried one. A lot of times different folks didn't want to carry them…

The boats were manned by two officers and one enlisted person. Officers because officers were briefed daily. We had daily intelligence briefings seven days a week, with the latest intelligence from the area. Or in the patrolling boat – officers would come back and debrief their area. So, the officers had a good feel for everything that was going in our area of operation and our sectors.

The enlisted person operated the motor. Now, this was my idea. And I went on each one of these – in command of each one that we did up to and including the night with Lieutenant Junior Grade Kerry.

I did that because it was my idea and people volunteered for this. And I didn't think it was right having one of these operations and being on a swift boat or back at Operations Center or something like that.

Myers: Because you thought it was a dangerous operation?

Schachte: Yes, and I had to be a part of it. It was my idea. The night in question, we-- as always, the swift boat would tow the skimmer out to the designated area. And we would board the skimmer. This night our call sign was 'Batman.' I got into the boat. My weapon was forward – the M-60 machine gun. John got in the boat. I don't remember who the enlisted person was. We then proceeded to the designated area. The swift boat would stay off, sometimes out of sight, sometimes not. But far enough away that they could ride shotgun on the mission.

Providing, also, long-ranged communications. All we had was this FM radio. We would then go into an area and as we did this night, shut the motor down and just drift. And we would drift along the shoreline or river bank or whatever it happened to be – looking for movement or listening for sounds of movement. This night, we were in an area – I recall we were so close to the beach you could actually hear the water lapping on the shoreline. It was between two and three in the morning – I don't remember. I detected what I thought was some movement. So, I took one of the hand-held flares and popped it instantly. It went up and when it burst – I don't know if you've heard that described, but it really lights up the area. I thought I saw the same area of movement. So, I opened up on it with my M-60.

Those guns were double loaded with tracers – Tango India, target identification. And John, right after I opened up, opened up with his M-16 and I could see he was firing in the direction of my tracer fire, which is why we had the double-loaded tracer. My gun jammed after the first burst and as I was trying to clear my weapon – John's gun apparently jammed too because he wouldn't fire anymore – I heard the old familiar, 'thump' – 'POW!'. And I looked, and John had fired the M-79 grenade launcher.

We were receiving NO fire from the beach. There were no muzzle flashes. The water wasn't boiling around the boat as it were – and the only noise was the noise we were making. So, I told the boat operator – the motor operator – to, you know, 'let's leave the area.' And we did, went back to port, eventually – went back to the swift boat and went back to port. And that morning, I went in and debriefed my commanding officer – our division commander, then Lieutenant Commander [Grant] 'Skip' Hibbard.

And I told him what happened. And I told him I was NOT going to be filing an after-action report, which is required if you have enemy action, because we had no enemy action. And I also after giving him all the details and I said, 'Oh, by the way – ' and I don't remember my exact words – 'John nicked himself with the M-79.' Those M-79s, by the way, have a kill radius of about five meters. A little over five yards. But, there is a shrapnel area beyond that. And that's what happened. And I was upset because that could have gone in somebody's eye and so on and so forth.

The division commander said, 'Fine, understand – no after-action report required.' Then, I found out that John had come in. And then I went back into a meeting and he had this small piece of shrapnel in his hand and he was requesting a Purple Heart. I was opposed to that. The division commander was opposed to that.

And John left our division four or five days later. I departed country maybe three weeks later. Skip left a few days after I left. So, we were all gone. And I forgot about it. Until some years later, someone told me

– and I don't recall who – to my surprise, John had been awarded a Purple Heart for that incident.

Fine, I felt I did my duty that night and that morning and it didn't bother me. And that's the way things were until about 20 years or so later. I was then an Admiral and I was in uniform – didn't have my hat on; I'd left that someplace in an office I was visiting. I was in the basement of the Senate Russell Office Building. And you have this subway system in the Capitol. I was waiting for a subway with a friend.

And he pointed – 'Look, that's Senator Kerry over there.' And I said, 'I know him.' And he said, 'You do?' And I hadn't seen or talked with John since Vietnam. And I guess I embarrassed my friend because I said, 'Hey, John!' Just like that. Well, he turned around, looked at me – it's about 20 paces away – and he kind of strolled over to me. And that call sign that night, if I haven't mentioned it, was 'Batman.' I think I have. But John walked over to me and got kind of close and he said, 'Batman.' And I was really impressed that he had that degree of recall. And, of course, we exchanged pleasantries. And we were going to do lunch. And, of course, we never did. And that was the last time I've seen him in person or been with him. And that went on. I retired – so on and so forth. And this March, I got a phone call from one of my swift boat colleagues, 'have you seen *Tour of Duty*?' [*the book,* Tour of Duty: John Kerry and the Vietnam War, *by Douglas Brinkley (William Morrow, 2004)*]

And I said, 'No, I certainly haven't.' ...And he said, 'Well, let me at least fax you these pages about an incident that we all you know you got personal information on and so on and so forth.' So, I said, 'Fine.' And he did. And I looked at that fax and read his account – and I was astonished. I'm not in the boat. The sampan issue and people and he's firing the hand-held grenade and so on and so forth. *[note: the account of the incident attributed to Kerry in Brinkley's book describes the mission encountering people in sampan vessels; Schachte recalls seeing no people or vessels]*

One other point: John was new in-country. He'd never been in a firefight. We never would – anybody with any combat experience will tell you – you would never assign somebody like that to an ambush mission like this, endangering, you know, other people if you didn't have some degree of experience.

We always had two officers in the boat.

No after-action report – no fire received and so and so forth. Well, I thank my friend for sending me that information. But I told him, 'Look, I'm not going to get involved in this.' You know, and I've heard from them and different people that they had a number of eyewitness reports on different things. And I just didn't want to expose my family to all of that. And I kind of maintained that posture—I'm not a member of the Swift Boat Veterans for Truth…

Myers: …are you saying that John Kerry accidentally injured himself?

Schachte: Yes. Clear-- of course, it was an accident.

Myers: That there was no enemy fire?

Schachte: There was no enemy fire—no after-action report, no muzzle flashes— nothing. No return fire from the beach at all.

Myers: So, in your view, he did not deserve the Purple Heart?

Schachte: That's what I told my commanding officer at the time.

Myers: And your commanding officer felt what?

Schachte: He agreed with me, after I related the story.

Myers: So, if you didn't support a Purple Heart and your commanding officer did not put in Kerry for a Purple Heart, how did he get it?

Schachte: You'll have to ask him. I don't know. And after—like I say, I had done my duty. It was over. I didn't care. I mean, that was not my issue. I was doing other things with my life.

Myers: Here's how John Kerry has described what happened that night. Quote: 'My M-16 jammed and as I bent down in the boat to grab another gun, a stinging piece of heat socked into my arm.' Is that accurate?

Schachte: It's accurate that his gun jammed, but it's not accurate (LAUGHS) that he was reaching something. He had already fired the M-79.

Myers: And that's what injured him?

Schachte: Yes.

Myers: It was an accidentally, self-inflicted wound?

Schachte: Yes, right. Which could have been very dangerous to any of the other two of us in that boat.

Myers: If you both were firing weapons how can you be absolutely certain that there was no enemy fire that hit John Kerry that night?

Schachte: Because when both guns jammed after the first burst, there was this moment of eerie silence until I heard the M-79 go off and the subsequent—almost immediate explosion from that weapon. And if you were there, (LAUGHS) you would know if you're being shot at, believe me.

Myers: …So what happens when you all return from the mission?

Schachte: We went back. I reported to the division commander. I debriefed him on what had happened that evening, earlier that morning. And that I was not going to file an after-action report because there was no enemy action. We received no fire from the beach and that John had gotten nicked from a round at—I don't remember my exact words. But, John had gotten nicked from an M-79 that he fired too close to the boat.

Myers: And there was no enemy fire involved?

Schachte: None.

Myers: Period?

Schachte: Yes.

Myers: You're absolutely certain?

Schachte: Yes.

Myers: 36 years later?

Schachte: Hey, listen, when somebody's shooting at you [LAUGHS], you know it. There was no—and some of the reasons you remember these things is because the starkness of what happens while that's going on…

Myers: You seem to be saying that John Kerry lied then and is lying today. That's a very serious charge. What proof do you have?

Swift Boats served the United States Navy well in Vietnam.

Schachte: The only thing that I can tell you—several things—number one, no after-action report, which would have been required. I was in command of those missions and I was in the boat that night. We always had two officers in the boat that night—in the boat when we did those operations, and an enlisted man on the motor. I saw no muzzle flashes or anything else. Now, that's what I saw. And it's not for me to judge what other people are going to think about that. That's up to other people.

Myers: But, you are, in a sense, saying Senator Kerry is lying and did not deserve his first Purple [Heart].

Schachte: I'm saying that he did not deserve the first Purple Heart from what I saw. You can characterize it anyway you want. But, I'm not going to say that.

Myers: Do you believe that John Kerry served honorably in Vietnam?

Schachte: Listen, everybody in that combat environment, as I said earlier, were all volunteers. I was only with him for this very small piece of that truncated tour that he had. I can only speak to what I saw that night and what-not. You have to ask others that spent more time with him. I couldn't give a judgment on something like that.

Myers: But, based on what you saw, do you believe John Kerry served honorably?

Schachte: From that night, from that incident, I would say that John Kerry sought a Purple Heart that was turned down that he later got. How he got it—I don't have a clue....

Myers: Do you believe that John Kerry showed courage?

Schachte: Listen, anybody on any of those boats at any time—I was there, we were there for Tet [*1968 Tet Offensive by North Vietnam and Vietcong forces*], and further times—you don't—you don't show up on the boat if—unless you've got a little bit of that in you.

Myers: Courage?

Schachte: Yes.

Myers: So, you're not saying that John Kerry was not courageous?

Schachte: No.

Myers: Or that he did not serve honorably?

Schachte: I can't judge that. All I can tell you about is that very brief period that I was with him on.

Myers: You say…that John Kerry was so new to country, there's no way you could have sent him out on a mission by himself?

Schachte: Yeah, not alone—in charge—no, uh-uh [negative].

Myers: Can you remember the name of the enlisted man that was with him?

Schachte: No. I really can't.

Myers: But, you're absolutely certain that John Kerry would not have been—never have been sent off in–

Schachte: Listen, my boss would not have permitted that, and neither would the chain of command. You just don't DO that on a mission on an ambush operation like this that's, um, dangerous, that dangerous. It's not fair to the person to put him in that situation. And it's not a situation of absolute necessity. We were just trying to turn the heat up. And that's why we sought volunteers. And that's why I went as a volunteer myself on these missions.

Myers: And John Kerry volunteered for that mission?

Schachte: Yep.

Myers: …What proof do you have that you were actually in that boat that night?

Schachte: Well, my report back to the division commander, the fact that we had officers in those boats, the fact that I was in the boat for those that we did up to and including that evening. And what I saw.

Myers: But, there's no documentation.

Schachte: No, listen, we're in a wartime environment. We didn't write up doctrines and stuff. We made the necessary reports – if you had a Casualty Report, After-Action Report, Operational Status of the Boats [Report], whether they were combat ready or not. I was responsible for all that as the operations officer. But, those are the kinds of things that we kept record of, records of.

Myers: And there would not have been any damage report on that…

Schachte: Correct, there was none—yeah.

Myers: The thing a lot of people are going to be asking Admiral is, it's been 35 years…

Schachte: Mm-hmm [affirmative].

Myers: Why speak out now in the heat of a presidential campaign?

Schachte: Well, the timing is something that's driven by the publication of *Tour of Duty*. As far as the timing is concerned, that was the precipitating thing that got those of us who were eyewitnesses, who served with John Kerry in Vietnam—made us aware of—of what he was saying. I was not interviewed by anybody for that book. Nor do I know anybody of my colleagues that were interviewed.

I'm non-partisan. Listen, I have voted Democrat, Republican. I voted for President Clinton the first time he ran. And I know what you're talking about. That has nothing to do—this is not a partisan issue. This is an issue of people stepping forward to tell their facts as they saw them.

Myers: John Kerry and two enlisted men insist they were on the boat that night and you were not. Why should we believe you?

Schachte: …there are two officers on each boat, each time we did one of these missions. I reported to the division command. I think he [*then-Lt.*

Cmdr. Grant Hibbard, Coastal Division 14] has been public with a sworn affidavit [*released by the organization Swift Boat Veterans for Truth*] as to my coming in to him and telling him what happened…

Myers: You think the two enlisted men are just making it up?

Schachte: I don't—I can't tell you anything about their motives. The only thing I can tell you is what I know, who I talked to about it—after the incident and—and that's all I can say…

Myers: Admiral, how can you be certain that John Kerry did not deserve that first Purple Heart?

Schachte: Well, other than the fact that I was in the boat with him when he fired this M-79 round too close to the boat and got nicked by it, I can't give you much more than that…

Myers: Can you think of anyone else who would recall your presence in the skimmer that day?

Schachte: Well, there are several people that may know the answer to that, and some of which have—one in particular has requested not to be involved. And I certainly honored that. Maybe someone who was in—the place where we—we stayed—after the incident. I think I said something to a couple of the guys, and they may have been able to remember the remark.

Myers: You said you went on, as I recall, that you went on nine different missions.

Schachte: Thereabouts. I'm not sure the number.

Myers: In this skimmer?

Schachte: Yeah, yeah.

Myers: Do you recall roughly where John Kerry's mission was in the sequence?

Schachte: It was the last one I went on. It was the last one I went on.

Myers: All right. And he went on only one.

Schachte: Yes. And then he departed about four days later to go South…

Myers: Why would John Kerry say that you weren't in the boat if you were?

Schachte: You'll have to ask John.

Myers: Can you think of a motive?

Schachte: Uh, I'll let you speculate. I'm not going to.

Myers: Is it possible in your view that John Kerry simply forgot that you were there?

Schachte: It could've been. I know he had vivid recollection of our call sign that night. It was repeated to me over 20 years later. But of course, that's possible.

Myers: …Everyone is going to wonder why now? Why come forward in the closing weeks of a presidential campaign. What is your motive?

Schachte: My only motive, as is the motive as I understand it of those brave eyewitness—witnesses that have come forward with sworn affidavits and what not –is to tell the truth. The timing was not in my control. The publication of his book and then the way he made this such an issue out of this whole campaign, his Vietnam service, and then some recent media discussions of all of those areas of his service that have been the matter of debate, my name has surfaced. And I just felt that it wasn't fair for me to continue to not—what I finally determined to be—to not do my duty, and just step forward, and say what I knew of that night, and not watch my colleagues continue to get beat up about he [I] wasn't there, and a lot of other things that I'm not even going to mention. In the print and the TV media.

Myers: …So you're not calling John Kerry a liar?

Schachte: All I'm telling you is what I know happened that night and who I told about it and what not… I'm not into name-calling. I just want to tell you what I knew that happened that night.

Myers: In your mind, John Kerry showed courage just going out on the mission.

Schachte: Sure.

Myers: You mentioned that you don't have a political motive. What have you done politically since you've been out of—retired from the Navy?…

Schachte: Yeah, well, I guess the first thing I did when I retired – I was working for the Mayor of Charleston who was running for Governor. He's a Democrat. And I was his statewide get-out-the-vote coordinator for that election. Unfortunately, we lost in the primary or in the primary runoff. I have contributed to Democratic Senators, one in particular from my own state. And have voted Democrat or Republican, depending on the person and the issues. I don't consider myself a partisan person. And I really haven't had any active involvement in politics other than that time when I was helping the person running for Governor in South Carolina in 1994.

Myers: What about President Bush?

Schachte: …First of all, let me tell you, I went to a number of rallies for Senator McCain, my wife and I. In fact, at the request of a longtime personal friend, I helped sponsor a luncheon for Senator McCain and made a financial contribution that went along with sponsorship. I did not go to the luncheon. And we were—I was discussing these matters with my wife. And finally decided that I—I was going to fully support George Bush. And before the election I got a call from a fellow general officer asking me if I was supporting Bush. And I said, "Yes, I was." And that I had contributed financially.

And he said they were going to put together a letter entitled 'Veterans for Bush.' And I said, 'I'll be glad to sign that letter, but only if I can edit it.' And of course, they agreed to that. And— that was really the extent of my active involvement with President Bush in the primary campaign.

Myers: You said you have contributed to him since you retired from the Navy?

Schachte: Yes, I have.

Myers: How much total?

Schachte: Total, I don't know. I gave him $1,000 when he ran the first time. And $1,000 so far this year.

Myers: Have you had any relationship or any contact with his campaign?

Schachte: Oh, absolutely not. I don't know that I know anybody in his campaign. And that, by the way, that's one thing that is really—it's difficult to get beyond those accusations that we're somehow puppets for this campaign. I mean that really strikes at the heart of your own personal honor. I mean I can't speak for others. And I've tried to keep that—or I shouldn't have said anything now. But—yeah, I know where you're going with that. But that answer's absolutely not.

Myers: So you're not doing this to help President Bush?

Schachte: For Lord's sake, no. Would I invite what's going to happen? (LAUGHS) I mean, I—no. Absolutely not.

Myers: …you've been around this town. I mean, why risk tarnishing your own reputation by wading into this morass?

Schachte: It is a matter of personal honor. I'm sorry. There are times in life when you have to do what you know is right regardless of the personal consequences.

Myers: You told me before that one of the reasons you wanted to—decided to speak out…is [because of] some of the things that were being said about you by the Kerry people on television…

Schachte: Well, that was the thing that pushed me over the side. But I'd rather not get involved in those specifics. I mean that in a sense is history. And I realize that I had to do my duty. I had to step up and be heard. Only on the only thing that I can talk about—which was this experience.

Myers: So you're not saying that John Kerry was, quote, 'unfit for command?'

Schachte: Listen, who is fit for command in the context of Commander-in-Chief is up to the American people to decide…

Myers: You said you are not a member of the Swift Boat Veterans for Truth.

Schachte: I admire them, but I'm not a member.

Myers: Okay. But you do support their cause.

Schachte: I support men that are willing to stand up and put up with what they've been putting up with just to tell the truth—of what they know to be the truth. And this is America. I mean that's what we do here.

Myers: Do you worry that your own reputation could be tarnished by getting involved in this?

Schachte: Oh, of course. Absolutely. And I knew that consequence was looking me dead in the face. But I also knew that it's not a higher calling. But there are times in life when you have to do what you know is right regardless of the personal consequences. And it's—it's not easy. And the reason I stayed out of this from the beginning is because I didn't want to get wrapped up into whatever kind of frenzy was going to follow. But I also knew that there were people who knew from what I told them of what happened that night. And I thought that would take care of it…

Myers: Some people will say, 'Look, you contributed money to the President's campaign.'

Schachte: Yeah.

Myers: Here it is the closing weeks of a very tight election. That this is all about politics.

Schachte: Well, see that's—that's probably the worst thing you could say to me. That I'm some kind of a political operative. That I would throw my reputation to the wolves to stand up for something that—as the inference is—is not true and expose my family to everything… I wouldn't do that. And I don't think anybody would do that.

Schachte reset the circumstance and the nudging emphasis of the interview well after the broadcast.

"I'm certain that what the journalists all want to do is force a result that will become a headline. In the case of the Lisa Myers interview, she was fair, and yet diligent in her mission. She pressed again and again for the headline she may have wanted. I resisted the badgering of the same question posed differently across the entire session. We took a few breaks and came back to it. The 2004 presidential election would likely be impacted. Sides were delineated. There were those who would believe the interview, those who would never believe the interview, and many independent voters in between," Schachte related.

"I hope all had the same conclusion that I did not want to be there or to interject my opinions in a very tight presidential race. It was not about that. It was about telling what I knew factually. I was apolitical. My conscience could only be at peace by telling the facts…telling the complete truth. Yet I did not want to be interview-directed to a headline that would read, 'Admiral calls Kerry a Liar.' That's exactly what the media wanted. I was not going to fall into the trap. My resolve was to tell the facts and let the listeners draw whatever conclusion they would from those facts. Politics carries too much emotion for too many," Schachte added.

Schachte's view of the interview and the result was not a point of pride, but a point of honor.

"I was uncomfortable being there, but I owed a duty to the people like Skip Hibbard, and all those that served and earned their awards. I knew that—at least Kerry's claim of that first Purple Heart—was not warranted from the first-hand action I witnessed. You don't forget those things. And I commanded every one of those 'skimmer op' exercises."

In the hard-fought 2004 campaign, both candidates received more votes than any previously elected president.[127]

"I did what I knew was right by speaking up when it was time to tell the truth. I can never regret that," Schachte resolved. "Whatever the election result would have been was not my purpose or mission. It was only about telling what I knew. History may judge us all one way, but God judges us the only way—by truth."

CHAPTER 20
What Next?

The Lisa Myers interview on NBC television opened other venues—all refused by the admiral. The media was at a frenzied pace trying to orchestrate controversy and confusion. Schachte remained steadfast in his convictions. In his brave step forward, he reminded the country that truth is the ultimate objective.

The daily calls became stifling. Schachte did not want to become the news. He only wanted to state the facts and let the public decide the future.

Columnist and talk show host Robert Novak also detailed Schachte's plight. He re-investigated the reports, the witnesses and the chronology of the SWIFT boat episode of August 2004 in his book, *Prince of Darkness*. In it, his reports clearly supported Schachte's assertions as a truthful witness. When the story broke, Kerry asserted that he was the only officer in the skimmer. Schachte, who detailed the origin of the mission and manned every one of the operations up to and beyond that time, corrected the senator. His commanding officer, Grant Hibbard, backed Schachte, as did many other witnesses—except two crewmen that appeared at the Democratic National Convention platform with Kerry. One would have to ask, "Why were they there?" Novak's book analyzed the episode from every angle and every possible witness. It became a compelling support case for Schachte.

There was another compelling case for the admiral's version that simplified the scenario to determine who was lying, based on common sense.

The "Antimedia Blogspot" from August of 2004 summarized the incident and pointed to Kerry as the fabricator with the help of a crewman.[128] The reprint below drew the conclusion to the 'blogspot' reader under a time-sensitive title.

"Rear Admiral Schachte breaks his Silence"

The blogspot unraveled the case for Admiral Schachte.

> *Robert Novak interviewed Rear Adm. Schachte who said in reference to the Swiftvets, "I didn't want to get involved." He changed his mind when his integrity was challenged by Democrats.*

> *"I was astonished by Kerry's version" (in his book, 'Tour of Duty') of what happened Dec. 2, Schachte said Thursday. When asked to support the Kerry critics in the Swift boat controversy, Schachte said, 'I didn't want to get involved.' But he said he gradually began to change his mind when he saw his own involvement and credibility challenged, starting with Lanny Davis on CNN's "Crossfire" Aug. 12.*

There is a startling revelation in Schachte's recollection of events.

Schachte, who also was then a lieutenant junior grade, said he was in command of the small Boston whaler or skimmer, with Kerry aboard in his first combat mission in the Vietnam War. The third crew member was an enlisted man whose name Schachte did not remember.

If there were only three men on that boat, and Schachte and Kerry were two of them, then either Patrick Runyon or Bill Zaladonis (or both) is lying about being there that night. This is astounding news! Schachte was the originator of the "Boston whaler" technique...two other former officers interviewed Thursday confirmed that Schachte was the originator of the technique and always was aboard the Boston Whaler for these missions. Grant Hibbard, who as a lieutenant commander was Schachte's superior officer, confirmed that Schachte always went on these skimmer missions and 'I don't think he (Kerry) was alone' on his first assignment. Hibbard said he had told Kerry to 'forget it' when he asked for a Purple Heart. Ted Peck confirms Schachte's recollection.

*Ted Peck, another Swift boat commander, said, "I remember Bill (Schachte) telling me it didn't happen" – that is, Kerry getting an enemy-inflicted wound. He said it would be "impossible" for Kerry to have been in the skimmer without Schachte. At this point, if the press really cared about the truth, both Pat Runyon and Bill Zaladonis would be questioned about their statements. One or the other **has to be lying** unless Schachte simply doesn't remember the second enlisted man (which would be amazing on a 14-foot boat). The truth is closing in on Kerry like a vise.*

This is astounding. History-in-the-making.

UPDATE: Rear Adm. Schachte was interviewed by Lisa Myers this evening, and we learned more of the details of the night of 2 Dec 68. It is now obvious that Bill Zaladonis is lying about being on the skimmer that night. Schachte said, "The boats were manned by two officers and one enlisted person," and "We always had two officers in the boat that night—in the boat when we did those operations, and an enlisted man on the motor." Furthermore, Schachte states, "I got into the boat. My weapon was forward – the M-60 machine gun. John got in the boat. I don't remember who the enlisted man was.

Zaladonis has claimed that he was manning the M-60 in the bow. This cannot be possible if there were always two officers on the boat and Schachte was manning the M-60. Both Runyon and Zaladonis were enginemen, so either one could have been manning the outboard motor. However, both also place Runyon on the motor and Zaladonis on the bow. Zaladonis **has to be lying** *about being on the boat that night. (And yes, I give full credit to the Admiral's version and none to Zaladonis. The facts all fit the Admiral's version—no after action report, both he and his CO refused Kerry's request for a Purple Heart, the attending physician testifies that Kerry had a piece of shrapnel that appeared to be from an M-79 grenade, Schachte, Hibbard and Peck all say that Schachte went on* **every** *"skimmer ops" mission, both Zaladonis and Runyon have changed their stories over time.)*

UPDATE 2: RADM Schachte has now released a statement as well.

UPDATE 3: If you're wondering what RADM Schachte's qualifications are, you can read a brief resume here. Suffice it to say he's an internationally recognized expert in the law of the sea.[129]

There was much more that came to the purview of the American voter. John Kerry spent only four months in Vietnam. When he returned to the United States, he became a war protestor. A summary of that activity was disseminated via "Truth or Fiction."[130] It was written by Vietnam Veteran Terry Garlock.

A young Kerry, however, broke faith with his brothers when he returned to the United States. With the financial aid of Jane Fonda, he led highly visible protests against the war. He wrote a book that many considered to be pro-Hanoi, titled "The New Soldier." The cover photo of his book depicted veterans in a mismatch of military uniforms mocking the legendary image of Marines raising the American flag atop Mount Suribachi in the 1945 battle for Iwo Jima, holding the American flag upside down. Kerry publicly supported Hanoi's position to use our POWs as a bargaining chip in negotiations for a peace agreement. Kerry threw what appeared to be his medals over a fence in front of the Capitol building in protest, on camera of course, but was caught in his lie years later when his medals turned up displayed on his office wall. Many good and decent people opposed the Vietnam War...But like Fonda's infamous visit to Hanoi in 1972, Kerry's public actions encouraged our enemy at a time they were killing America's sons. Decades after the war was done, interviews with our former enemy's leaders confirmed that public protests in the United States, like Kerry's, played a significant role in their strategy. Many of us wonder which of our brothers who died young would be alive today had people like Fonda and Kerry objected to the war in a more suitable way.[131]

Finally, the voice of reason arrived in the form of a well-researched *Patriot's Post* presentation.

"A new voice has been added to the debate over the circumstances surrounding Sen. John Kerry's first Purple Heart. William Schachte, who was a lieutenant in the Navy during Kerry's Vietnam tour - and who later rose to the rank of Rear Admiral - has released a statement describing the events of December 2-3, 1968, when Kerry received a minor shrapnel wound for which he was awarded the Purple Heart. What follows is Schachte's statement, in full."[132]

The Bill Schachte statement described the full sequence.

"I volunteered to serve in Vietnam and was assigned to Coastal Division 14 for a normal tour of duty. I was a Lieutenant serving as Operations Officer and second in command at Coastal Division 14 when Lieutenant (junior grade) John Kerry reported to us in mid-November 1968. Lt. (jg) Kerry was an Officer-in-Charge (O-in-C) under training in preparing to be assigned as one of our Swift Boat O-in-C's.

"At some point following President Johnson's announcement of the suspension of bombing in North Vietnam in March 1968, we were directed to become more aggressive in seeking to find and destroy or disrupt the enemy in our operating area. As part of this effort, I conceived a new operation that became known as 'Skimmer OPS.' The concept was simple. A 15-foot Boston Whaler was sent into an area where, based on coordinated intelligence, North Vietnamese cadre and Viet Cong were expected to be meeting or where, for example, concentrations of enemy forces might be involved in the movement of arms or munitions. We were to draw fire and quickly get out of the area. This would allow more concentrated firepower to be brought against the enemy forces we had been able to identify.

"These operations were carried out only in "hot" areas and well away from any villages or populated areas. A Swift Boat would tow the skimmer to the general area of operations, and the ambush team would then board the skimmer and proceed to the designated area of operations. The Swift Boat would be riding shotgun and standing off, occasionally out of sight, to provide fire support and long-range communications. The Skimmer was powered by an outboard motor, and we carried an FM radio, handheld flares, an M-60 machine gun with a bipod mount, and an M-16 mounted with a starlight scope. If the night was heavily overcast, we brought an M-14 mounted with an infrared scope. We also carried an M-79 single-shot grenade launcher. In addition to our combat gear and flak jackets, we often carried .38-caliber pistols.

"The operation consisted of allowing the skimmer to drift silently along shorelines or riverbanks to look or listen for sounds of enemy activity. If activity was identified, we would open fire with our automatic weapons, and if we received fire, we would depart the area as quickly as possible, leaving it to air support or mortar fire from a Swift Boat standing off at a distance to carry out an attack.

"I commanded each of these Skimmer operations up to and including the one on the night in question involving Lt. (jg) Kerry. On each of these operations, I was in the skimmer manning the M-60 machine gun. I took with me one other officer and an enlisted man to operate the outboard motor. I wanted another officer because officers, when not on patrol, were briefed daily on the latest intelligence concerning our sector of operations and were therefore more familiar with the current intelligence. Additionally, at these daily briefings, officers debriefed on their patrol areas after returning to port.

"On the night of December 2-3, we conducted one of these operations, and Lt. (jg) Kerry accompanied me. Our call sign for that operation was "Batman." I have no independent recollection of the identity of the enlisted man, who was operating the outboard motor. Sometime during the early morning hours, I thought I detected some movement inland. At the time we were so close to land that we could hear water lapping on the shoreline. I fired a hand-held flare, and upon it bursting and illuminating the surrounding area, I thought I saw movement. I immediately opened fire with my M-60. It jammed after a brief burst. Lt. (jg) Kerry also opened fire with his M-16 on automatic, firing in the direction of my tracers. His weapon also jammed. As I was trying to clear my weapon, I heard the distinctive sound of the M-79 being fired and turned to see Lt. (jg) Kerry holding the M-79 from which he had just launched a round. We received no return fire of any kind nor were there any muzzle flashes from the beach. I directed the outboard motor operator to clear the area.

"*Upon returning to base, I informed my commanding officer, Lt. Cmdr. Grant Hibbard, of the events, informing him of the details of the operation and that we had received no enemy fire. I did not file an "after action" report, as one was only required when there was hostile fire. Soon thereafter, Lt. (jg) Kerry requested that he be put in for a Purple Heart as a result of a small piece of shrapnel removed from his arm that he attributed to the just-completed mission. I advised Lt. Cmdr. Hibbard that I could not support the request because there was no hostile fire. The shrapnel must have been a fragment from the M-79 that struck Lt. (jg) Kerry, because he had fired the M-79 too close to our boat. Lt. Cmdr. Hibbard denied Lt. (jg) Kerry's request. Lt. (jg) Kerry detached our division a few days later to be reassigned to another division. I departed Vietnam approximately three weeks later, and Lt. Cmdr. Hibbard followed shortly thereafter. It was not until years later that I was surprised to learn that Lt. (jg) Kerry had been awarded a Purple Heart for this night.*

"*I did not see Lt. (jg) Kerry in person again for almost 20 years. Sometime in 1988, while I was on Capitol Hill, I ran into him in the basement of the Russell Senate Office Building. I was at that time a Rear Admiral and in uniform. He was about 20 paces away, waiting to catch the underground subway. In a fairly loud voice, I called out to him, "Hey, John." He turned, looked at me, came over and said, "Batman!" We exchanged pleasantries for a few minutes, agreed to have lunch sometime in the future, and parted ways. We have not been together since that day.*

"*In March of this year, I was contacted by one of my former swift boat colleagues concerning Douglas Brinkley's book about Senator Kerry, 'Tour of Duty.' I told him that I had not read it. He faxed me a copy of the pages relating to the action on the night of December 2-3, 1968. I was astonished by Senator Kerry's rendition of the facts of that night. Notably, Lt. (jg) Kerry had himself in charge of the operation, and I was not mentioned at all. He also claimed that he was wounded by hostile fire.*

"None of this is accurate. I know, because I was not only in the boat, but I was in command of the mission. He was never more than several feet away from me at any time during the operation that night. It is inconceivable that any commanding officer would put an officer in training, who had been in country only a couple of weeks, in charge of such an ambush operation. Had there been enemy action that night, there would have been an after-action report filed, which I would have been responsible for filing.

"I have avoided talking to media about this issue for months. But, because of the recent media attention, I felt I had to step up to recount my personal experiences concerning this incident."[133]

Schachte's details of that late night – early morning incident have never changed. Even the detail of Senator Kerry's reference to their call-sign, "Batman," many years later re-supported the incident. It was Kerry's only "Skimmer Ops" activity. And Schachte reminds those–many blinded by political motivation—that the truth draws 'the fire of ire,' and that he commanded every Skimmer Ops mission.

"There would be no circumstance that would have me (Schachte) the skipper (Grant Hibbard) send in an inexperienced junior unaccompanied," Schachte recalled. "I was on every mission—period."

One could walk many miles in a single day under the U.S. Capitol. There are maps and signage to guide one to the three House of Representatives office buildings. There are underground thoroughfares to the three Senate office buildings, as well. Staffers dart to and fro. There are military uniforms moving from one large solid wooden door to the next. The weather outside remains unimposing and of no consequence. The clocks have lighted indicators as warning signals for attendance—and votes.

Personal staff, committee staff, leadership staff, institutional staff, and support agency staff members number into the thousands.[134] Conference rooms and committee rooms empty and populate by a symphonic staging that only those minions can command. There are lobbyists and photographers, tour guides, pages, and coffee clerks. And as one walks from one hallway to the next, there are endless indications of the security required. A visitor is apt to notice one familiar face from the news—or a dozen.

One could see the nightly faces—Nancy Pelosi, Jim Jordan, Tom Cotton, Chuck Schumer, Lindsey Graham, and...former Senator and Secretary of State John Kerry. They walk those wide hallways, too. They generally keep their eyes ahead while listening to their chief-of-staff or their director of national security. They are on their way to a vote, an interview, or a hearing. Our country is in their hands.

One would not likely see the Charleston rear admiral, Bill Schachte, there these days. He is at home volunteering, mentoring, and praying. He prefers it that way. He is in a pace of life he controls.

CHAPTER 21
In God's Hands

Schachte had always been attentive to his faith. His career was part of it. His marriage to Carmen strengthened their walk of faith, together. As his career responsibilities ebbed, his faith became evermore his "work."

"I once met a Catholic monsignor in Washington, DC, whose father was chief of Naval Operations. He asked me how I selected an executive assistant. I told him it was very simple for me. I knew the community—having been the Director of Personnel of the entire JAG Corps at one time. I would go around and pick someone smarter than me and interview him. I would then get them to follow me around. The monsignor seemed astonished at my routine. He said, 'This is Washington, DC, and you admit to me that you would admit to others that there were others who were smarter than you?' I laughed and said, 'That's the way it is—I have no pretensions. In the performance of my duties I need the best I can get.'"

After his selection to Admiral, Schachte had the occasion to become involved in the study of the Bible. He joined a prayer group which met at the Pentagon.

"The 'flag' (admirals and generals) officer Bible fellowship that I participated in every Thursday in the Army Executive Mess began after the announcement of my promotion to admiral. Doctor Soderquist, our leader, was a member of the Christian Embassy affiliated with Doctor Bill Bright's 'Campus Crusade for Christ.' It was an interdenominational group of men and women—all admirals or generals.

"In 1992, and by Soderquist's recommendation, I began reading the Bible nightly before going to sleep. I use a 'daily' Bible which has Old Testament,

New Testament, Proverbs, and Psalms laid out in daily increments so one could go through the entire Bible in one year. I have been doing that every night since I began in 1992. It has become a real ritual in my life and very relaxing last thing to do in the evening," the admiral divulged.

Schachte became even more engaged. He wanted to assist others in their life's journey. His personal spirituality was not going to remain his secret. It was to be shared.

Schachte elaborated, "I once spoke at a breakfast in downtown D.C. to a group of business executives. I was happy to be there and spoke about my personal walk of faith. Later, I made several other speeches around the country—and though political expediency seemed to become an obstacle—I never backed away from the key themes in my life—faith, family, and fairness."

The nuance of speaking to others about the importance of the Bible, and its lessons applied to everyday life, beckoned. It became a passion.

"When my selection to Admiral was announced I received a number of invitations to different events. One that caught my eye was an invitation to a bible fellowship sponsored by a group known as the Christian Embassy. So, I went to flag protocol and checked them out and learned that they were a respected group of admirals and generals who had a weekly bible study in the Pentagon. I accepted the invitation to join them but was unable to make the first meeting. The speaker, interestingly, was former South Dakota Governor Joe Foss, but I was out of town on travel. He was a Marine pilot and the leading combat ace of World War II. He was a Medal of Honor recipient, as well. Though I missed hearing him, we would meet later.

"Eventually I was invited to give some speeches on my faith. There were a couple of other Catholics in our group; there was one fellow who was a Greek Orthodox, and some Baptists, and an Episcopalian. It was really an impressive inter-denominational group.

"After becoming an Admiral, one benefit was having the ability to have an executive assistant or an 'EA' as an aide. I had a number of extremely and extraordinarily talented young JAG lawyers serve with me as my EA. And, interestingly, each one who served as an EA with me retired as an admiral, except one, and that was a very large disappointment. Having had that experience with executive assistants, I keenly followed their careers. I wanted to influence each of them in a positive way and believe that I was able to do so.

"I tried to work with my executive assistants from the perspective of giving them what we would call in the Navy 'a view from the bridge.' In other words, seeing our community from the position of the person responsible. At the time I was the acting JAG, we had over 1,100 Navy lawyers, men and women, stationed around the world. I would have the EAs follow me around to various commands and tried to lead by example. And, as they probably well knew, I learned from them, too." Schachte summarized.

In fact, Schachte's impact on his sailors was profound, in large part because of the sincere and deeply-felt care he had for those under him, especially his assigned personal staff. That sincerity cannot be faked over the long haul. One executive assistant, retired Navy Captain Dan McCarthy, sees Schachte as a life-mentor and had the following praise for the man: "Admiral Schachte demonstrated his concern for us during our service together in a rare way. He wrote note cards or made calls home to our spouses to explain why he needed to keep us working at the office late into the evening hours and sometimes on weekends. This work pace is common in the Pentagon but is rarely appreciated in the genuine way Bill Schachte expressed it. Most Admirals are demanding, and it's always about them. Not Admiral Schachte. He empowered me by inclusion. He could be in the middle of big things, and would stop all to ask me how my son played in his little league game or how my daughter was doing in school. He made my family and friends, his family and friends. Thirty years later nothing's changed. He still calls to check on me, and express his interest in my life, family and friends. I am as appreciative and loyal now, as I was then. He earned my respect, and has always been the epitome of a principled servant-leader. That's love, and it was all too often missing among many top leaders in the services, civilian or military." As if that praise were not enough, McCarthy added, "That temporary father-son relationship we had, which ended formally at the end of our tour, continues to this day!" 1977 Naval Academy graduate Dan McCarthy ought to know, he later served as legal advisor to Secretary of the Navy John H. Dalton for nearly six consecutive years during the Clinton Presidency.

"One never stops learning," the admiral observed. "And you're never too old."

In addition to his close work with his executive assistants and active participation in the organized Bible studies, Schachte accepted many speaking engagements.

"I accepted an invitation to speak at the annual Mayor's Prayer Breakfast in Cape Girardeau, Missouri. It is the largest mayoral prayer breakfast in America. There were 1,200 people present for my speech, and it was quite an experience. I had spoken before on the importance of faith. Perhaps someone heard me, and the invitation to the prestigious breakfast became a reality. I was totally humbled to be asked," the admiral added.

"Soon after retiring, I spoke at another mayor's prayer breakfast in Augusta, Georgia. This was a fine group and I found that these testimonies were as beneficial to me as they were to the audience. They gave me an insight into the many personal blessings of my life.

"The Cape Girardeau event was after the Augusta event. It was their ninth annual Mayor's Prayer Breakfast and the event grew in stature annually. I looked at the distinguished list of previous Cape Girardeau keynote speakers. They had Adolph Coors, IV; the soccer star Kyle Rote, Jr.; Bob Vernon, Los Angeles Police Chief; then Bill Armstrong, former U.S. Senator from Colorado; Dave Dravecky, former pitcher of the San Francisco Giants; Cal Thomas, the nationally-syndicated columnist; and Charles Duke, the astronaut. That was the year before my presentation. I spoke in 1996.

"My theme in all my presentations was that life is not about finding your destiny but instead it is the journey for peace and balance that can only be found by a relationship with Jesus Christ," Schachte stated. "We often confuse ourselves."

He recalled the Missouri theme.

"I took advantage of an opportunity in Cape Girardeau to quote Adolph Coors who spoke at the first Mayor's Prayer Breakfast in 1988. He said, 'Outside the will of God there is no success, but in the will of God there is no failure.' Indeed, my Catholic faith has been the mainstay of my adult life—and I'm blessed with my loving and faithful wife, Carmen and our family."

He transitioned to his own circumstances.

"Speaking of faith—one of my favorite biblical verses is from the Gospel of Mark when a man was pleading with our Lord to free his child from a demon. I quote here now from Mark 9:23 Jesus said to him, 'All things are possible to him who believes.' Next verse, 9:24, 'Immediately the father of the child cried out and said in tears, Lord I believe, help me in my unbelief.' I read this passage because I find it personally meaningful. This is a powerful message."

Many read the Bible. Few internalize it like the admiral. He searches the words to find the deeper and more apropos modern application.

Admiral Billy Schachte as a Featured Speaker at Prayer breakfast. Phot courtesy Schachte Family Archives.

"There is another passage that I think is very appropriate and that is from the Psalms 37:4: 'Delight yourself in the Lord and he shall give you the desires of your heart.' Faith is a choice—not an argument. It is a decision—not a debate. It is a commitment and not a controversy. Faith fulfils some need in your heart. It can be defined as wanting more out of life. As Billy Graham often pointed out, 'Even those with incredible wealth realize that their social standing and wealth leave a void in their lives.' He continued, "As Saint Augustine once said, 'Our souls are restless until they rest in thee.' As human beings, we suspect that out there somewhere there is always something more, and where does this intuition from something more come from? I believe it is built into our nature. Human beings are termed as an incredibly religious animal by instinct, and I believe that to be true."

"Another favorite is Proverbs 3:5-6, which I had printed on the back of my retirement program handout. 'Trust in the LORD with all your heart and lean not on your own understanding; in all your ways acknowledge Him, and he will direct your paths.' It is a favorite because it should guide every life."

Schachte returned to the early basis of his faith—a loving family life in his Charleston youth. When he lost his dad, he was able to put it all in perspective.

"It was at my dad's funeral where, in his concluding remarks for my dad's eulogy, our pastor Monsignor Manning stated in his last sentence, 'Bill Schachte is not gone, he lives on in his children.' Later that day after everyone had left my mother's home, and I was alone. I vowed that I would never again miss a Sunday Mass nor go to church where I would not be in a position to receive communion. I followed that since 1970. Being human, I have had a few circumstances that required that I miss. I missed it very few times."

Later, in 1972, I began making New Year's resolutions and writing them down. 1972 was the year that I quit smoking. When it came to Thanksgiving in 1972, I realized that I only had a little while to go so I quit at Thanksgiving time, no pun intended, 'cold turkey.' I never went back to smoking. I don't miss it at all."

Less than four years earlier, Schachte had his family with him—Carmen and little Billy, along with his father and mother—when he stood on the tarmac at the Charleston Air Force Base getting ready to board a plane.

He was heading to Swift Boat School in Coronado before his tour of duty in Vietnam.

"When I boarded that plane at Charleston for California and SWIFT Boat training, Carmen and Billy stayed in the airport for goodbyes. We were planning to rejoin in San Diego after I could locate a place for us to stay. My Mom and Dad walked with me to the tarmac, as we boarded outdoors back then. My mother then gave me a big hug and said, 'Billy, may Our Lord hold you in the palm of His Hand.' Those words choked me up. My Dad grabbed my shoulder, winked and said, 'That's okay, Billy.' He saw that I was saddened that I might never see them again. I made my way walking alone to the stairs for the plane. It was a lonely flight across the country—and lonelier yet when I left for Vietnam. It would be enough to keep God in your life every day."

More than fifty years hence, the admiral still enjoys the time to find personal insights and to say daily prayers. He also tries to remember an insight. "No matter where he is or what time it is, God's always my audience."

There is a quiet comfort in reaching the reflective stages of life knowing that it was lived correctly and with an inherent zest for the spiritual life beyond. Schachte has had several difficult physical issues over the latter years but has always turned to the truth. The truth compels all else. His truth is that there is someone greater and more important that has watched over him for a lifetime—from dangerous military missions, to a Viet Cong sniper, to the requisite needs one incurs with aging. He believes. It matters.

"Reflecting on my life, my most difficult nights were when I tried to go to sleep after learning earlier that afternoon that my father had died suddenly and that foreboding time before I was scheduled 'as a volunteer' to leave Carmen and Billy to board a flight for a tour of combat duty in Vietnam. There were others, but these two nights stood out.

A lifetime of teamwork with Carmen was essential. They moved often because of the military commitments and those related to Schachte's later legal career. They raised both boys to capable and productive young men. They reconnected with many friends—from the Navy, the Pentagon, law school, and from Schachte's Charleston childhood. They had even more in Puerto Rico.

The Schachtes celebrated their 50th Wedding anniversary in 2015. It was truly a special night with many friends and family, held at the Country Club of Charleston. He demonstrated his devotion to his wife that night. Carmen's devotion was equally impressive.

The retired admiral told of crucial moments in their lives. Carmen proved to have excellent intuition. That quality made a difference.

"In fact, she has been a lifesaver," Schachte intimated in perspective.

"Carmen saved my life more than once," the admiral recounted. "After an extended Thanksgiving weekend when we had a number of house guests, all had left. Carmen went back to our bedroom early—around 6:30. It was an exhausting weekend. I went upstairs around 7:00 p.m. to go to bed. When I got to the top stairs there was a huge plastic bag full of trash. I didn't want Carmen to wake up in the morning to go downstairs and see that trash bag still sitting there. I decided to bring it downstairs. It was a very good bag, no tears but a lot of stretches. Unfortunately, the first step I took was on one of those stretched areas of the bag, and I went bouncing down the stairs—two levels and 22 steps. I got all the way to the bottom and was unable to get up off the floor. I called out to Carmen to help because I had fallen hard and was injured," he recalled.

Schachte was in tremendous pain. The retired sailor mustered a resolve to get to help by waking his bride, despite the strain. It was a "mind over matter" experience.

"I realized that she was sleeping—and she sleeps very soundly. So, I crawled over to the stanchion by the stairs pulled myself up and then walked up to the two flights of stairs to her side of our bed. She looked up at me and said, 'What was that noise?' I responded it was me falling down the stairs to which she replied, 'And you walked up the stairs and you are standing here talking to me, take a hot shower, and we will discuss it in the morning.' I then told her that the right side of my back as on fire," Schachte retold.

"She woke up and got dressed and drove me to an overnight facility where a CT scan was performed, and it was discovered that I had four fractured ribs on my right side. I was then taken by ambulance to the hospital trauma ward. I was kept for a couple of days at the Medical University of South Carolina Hospital."

He recalled yet another dangerous episode when wife Carmen reacted and did what was necessary.

"She saved me again. On December 23, 2016, I had been on the phone with my brother, Frank, talking about dinner arrangements for Christmas Day. Suddenly, I couldn't get my words out properly. Carmen happened to be walking by and took the phone out of my hand and told Frank, 'I'll call you later.' She then turned to me and said, 'Put on your jacket, I am taking you to the hospital and I am driving.' I, of course protested. I looked at her inquisitively, and I muttered, 'Hospital?' She had made up her mind."

Her instincts mattered profoundly.

"She said, 'Yes, shut up and get in the car, and I am driving.' We did and by the time I got to the hospital we learned that I was in the early stages of a hemorrhagic stroke, or a major brain bleed which I was later told had been occasioned by taking blood thinners over the years for my atrial fibrillation condition. I was in the ICU for four days and was then discharged to home. It took me a while to get back to a semblance of normal and everyone told me that if not for my wife's quick action the stroke would have been fatal. As it turned out, my cognition tests were passed after only three sessions. Likewise, my mobility test was proven acceptable after only four sessions, but with residual balancing issues. I was lucky. Better said, I was lucky to have Carmen."

The Schachte marriage has been an active one. The "home for the admiralty" is on Charleston's Broad Street, just two blocks from their faith-centered Cathedral of St. John the Baptist. They often stay at their cottage on Kiawah Island to enjoy long morning walks on the pristine South Carolina beachfront. They also own a condominium in Puerto Rico where the popular couple returns often to visit Carmen's family. That home sustained much damage from Hurricane Maria in September of 2017.[135]

"That hurricane devastated the island. The direct and indirect deaths in the aftermath of the horrific storm were misreported. There is still much to do on the island to restore it to pre-storm conditions. Carmen and I have visited several times after the storm. We both have a special place in our hearts for the people of Puerto Rico. Many are family."

It is true that in every great marriage there is a synergy that propels a couple to exist as a unit to a common destiny of happiness and a mindset of compassionate care. The Schachte marriage has been based on an exceptional value system that has compelled them to thrive through the adventures...and the misadventures.

Schachte reflected upon the year apart when everything was about duty in the face of an enemy, the wartime media interpretations, and the next day that could be crossed out from a wall calendar so that he could rejoin Carmen and little Billy.

He returned. He found other advancement within new opportunities—and he achieved an honorable life borne of the hardships of the past.

"Had it not been for my faith and Carmen, these difficulties could not have been placed where they belonged—as my mother whispered—in God's hands."

Carmen & Billy with grandchildren Liam (center) and Gunnar (right). Photo courtesy Schachte family archives.

Postscript

Clemson University presented Admiral Schachte with an honorary Doctor of Law Degree. It was unexpected.

"One of the most humbling experiences in my career occurred in 1999. I received a call from the President of Clemson University telling me that the faculty and board of trustees had voted to award me an honorary Doctor of Laws Degree.

"I guess it is routine, but he asked me if I would accept. That took about one nanosecond for me to say, 'Yes, I am so terribly honored, not only for me but for my family of Clemson graduates. I later learned that there was only one other honorary degree awarded at that ceremony, a person who flew in from Tokyo. He was an executive vice president of Fuji Films International Operations.

"While on the phone with President Curris, he told me there would also be a luncheon. I could invite a certain number of people to join me.

I told him I would get back to him with some names--which I did. He then asked if I had any other special requests. I laughed and said, 'Only one. Please do all you can to make sure my fraternity brothers do not find out about this award.' I didn't want the school to have a demonstration on their hands," Schachte retold with a grin.

TRUTH ACROSS THE WATERS

William L. Schachte, Jr., Rear Admiral, U.S. Navy (Ret.)

Born in Charleston, South Carolina, Rear Admiral Bill Schachte graduated from Clemson University and the University of South Carolina School of Law. Rear Admiral Schachte's distinguished United States Naval career as a line officer, and later as an attorney, included a volunteer combat tour in Vietnam on small boats and service as the Judge Advocate General. In 1992, he was awarded the Order of the Palmetto by then Governor Carroll Campbell. In 1993, Schachte retired from the United States Navy to live in South Carolina. Real Admiral Schachte is a member of the South Carolina *Hunley* Commission.

Rear Admiral Schachte stated: "The *Hunley* was the first submersible to prove the advantage of using submarine technology for military purposes; our current submarine force is a vital element that is utilized by our nation to ensure our security and the freedom of the seas. The year 2000 marks the one-hundredth anniversary of the United States submarine force. The submarine force of today primarily consists of 58 fast-attack and 18 TRIDENT ballistic missile submarines. Fast-attack submarines operate as one of the most flexible platforms in the Navy, performing anti-submarine warfare, anti-surface warfare, land attack, mine laying, intelligence gathering, and the delivery of special forces, all without ever being seen. The newest addition to the submarine force and the fast-attack fleet is the USS *Seawolf*. As the most survivable asset in our country's strategic triad, TRIDENT submarines carry more than half of the nation's strategic arsenal. Although purposely unseen while operating at sea, submarines will continue to be the silent but highly effective force protecting this country for at least the next one-hundred years."

Clemson University Honorary Degree Citation.

"The graduation ceremony and award presentation were very memorable. A photo of President Curris, me, and the other recipient was printed in a local newspaper the next day. President Curris later left Clemson University to work in Washington, D.C.

"Unfortunately, my mother was in an assisted living facility and could not join us. So, the next day our family went to see her and brought a video of the pertinent part of the ceremony to show to her. It was really very nice holding her hand while watching the short video. She was a major catalyst of my education and career—and her background was in education, as well."

The citation for Admiral Schachte's Doctor of Laws Honorary Degree at Clemson University was presented at their commencement exercises of May 1999. It summarizes a life lived in truth.

The formal presentation is reprinted below.

TRUTH ACROSS THE WATERS

Rear Admiral William L. Schachte, Jr.

A Life of Law in Service to His Country

Clemson	1963
OCS	1964
Vietnam Volunteer	1968
Officer SWIFT boat PCF45	
Executive/Operations Officer	
NROTC Instructor, University of Rochester	
Law degree, University of South Carolina	1973
Master of Laws, George Washington University	1979
Deputy Assistant JAG, JAG community manager	1984
Appointed Rear Admiral Lower Half,	1988
Assistant JAG of the Navy	
Commander, Naval CIS Command	
Promoted to Rear Admiral Upper Half	1990
Appointed Acting Judge Advocate General, Navy	1992

Placard Archive from Schachte Family. This printing accompanied a speaking engagement for a distinguished Congressman after Rear Admiral Schachte's 1993 retirement.

RADM Bill Schachte with wife Carmen at a formal event. Photo courtesy Schachte Family Archives.

About the Author

W. Thomas McQueeney is the author of ten books in genres that include history, literary humor, biographical topics, and a novel. He is a 1974 graduate of The Citadel and serves myriad philanthropic community endeavors. McQueeney has been familiar with the Schachte family prowess over his lifetime.

The author is a recipient of the Order of the Palmetto, the highest civilian award conferred upon a citizen of his native state, South Carolina. He serves as Chairman of the Congressional Medal of Honor Museum Foundation, Inc. charged with building the $50 million National Medal of Honor Leadership & Education Center at Patriots Point in Mount Pleasant. He is married and has four children and four grandchildren.

Author W. Thomas McQueeney. Photo by Amanda McQueeney, wife of the author.

Endnotes

1 Siege of Charleston. http://www.sonofthesouth.net/leefoundation/civil-war/1863/siege-of-charleston.htm

2 1790 Census. https://www.census.gov/history/www/through_the_decades/overview/1790.html

3 1860 Census. https://www.censusrecords.com/content/1860_Census

4 1960 Census. https://www.censusrecords.com/content/1860_Census

5 Charleston Navy Yard. http://www.scencyclopedia.org/sce/entries/charleston-naval-shipyard/

6 Anderson College beginnings. https://snaccooperative.org/ark:/99166/w6bw2djs

7 IBID.

8 Winthrop College. https://www.winthrop.edu/aboutus/history/

9 College of Charleston history. https://www.cofc.edu/about/historyandtraditions/briefhistory.php

10 Pittsfield GE Plant. https://www.wbur.org/radioboston/2016/06/29/ge-and-pittsfield

11 Sacred Heart Church Charleston, SC. https://www.sacredheartcharleston.org

12 Summerville, SC. https://www.summervillesc.gov/?SEC=F7F9A53F-DD55-4A78-B29E-8D81FAA8C799

13 Henry Schachte born 1850. https://www.findagrave.com/memorial/46866874/henry-schachte

14 IBID.

15 Mayor Joseph P. Riley, Jr. https://www.npr.org/2016/01/09/462400074/americas-longest-serving-mayor-steps-down

16 Joseph Cardinal Bernardin. https://www.britannica.com/biography/Joseph-Louis-Cardinal-Bernardin

17 IBID.

18 Thomas Green Clemson. https://www.clemson.edu/about/history/

19 John C. Calhoun. https://www.britannica.com/biography/John-C-Calhoun

20 Opening of Clemson College. https://www.britannica.com/biography/John-C-Calhoun

21 John Heisman. https://clemsontigers.com/landmark-events-in-tiger-history-hiring-of-john-heisman/

22 Clemson University History. https://www.britannica.com/topic/Clemson-University

23 IBID.

24 IBID.

25 IBID.

26 Harvey Gantt. http://www.scencyclopedia.org/sce/entries/gantt-harvey/

27 Order of the Palmetto. https://www.sciway.net/hist/sc-order-of-the-palmetto.html

28 Lorain County name. http://www.hullnumber.com/LST-1177

29 Lorain county, Ohio. IBID.

30 Lorain County retirement. IBID.

31 Admiral John S. McCain. http://www.arlingtoncemetery.net/jsmccain.htm

32 IBID.

33 John S. McCain III. https://www.c-span.org/person/?johnmccain

34 Prussian History. https://www.britannica.com/place/Prussia

35 Famous Prussians in history. https://www.historytoday.com/archive/kingdom-prussia-founded

36 Tailhook Association. https://www.tailhook.net/reunion

37 Tailhook date and location. https://www.tailhook.net/reunion

38 Map of Cam Ranh Bay. https://www.google.com/search?q=map+cam+ranh+bay&client=safari&rls=en&tbm=isch&source=iu&ictx=1&fir=gqIfpur6XLUqSM%253A%252C8VaCmdY2o-MHGM%252C_&vet=1&usg=AI4_-kRuvVwrvuZquCW3jISn3-S3YMwisHA&sa=X&ved=2ahUKEwjg56ScoaToAhWMZd8KHeD1ALIQ9QEwAnoECAoQGA

39 Skunk Alpha Encounter. https://www.nytimes.com/2017/07/14/opinion/the-skunk-alpha-encounter.html

40 IBID.

41 IBID.

42 Flank Speed. https://www.abbreviations.com/Flank%20speed

43 Douglas AC 47. https://aircraftnut.blogspot.com/2014/05/ac-47-dakota-gunship-spooky-and-puff.html

44 Douglas AC 47. https://aircraftnut.blogspot.com/2014/05/ac-47-dakota-gunship-spooky-and-puff.html

45 PCF Swift Boat. https://www.militaryfactory.com/ships/detail.asp?ship_id=Swift-Boat-PCF

46 PCF Swift Boat. https://www.militaryfactory.com/ships/detail.asp?ship_id=Swift-Boat-PCF

47 End of Vietnam War. https://www.history.com/topics/vietnam-war/vietnam-war-timeline

48 Dustoff Medevac. http://www.chuckandlorene.com

49 IBID.

50 Tet Offensive. https://www.answers.com/Q/How_many_American_soldiers_died_in_the_tet_offensive

51 Martin Luther king Assassination. https://www.history.com/topics/black-history/martin-luther-king-jr-assassination

52 IBID.

53 IBID.

54 Robert Kennedy Assassination. https://www.history.com/this-day-in-history/bobby-kennedy-is-assassinated

55 Democratic National Convention. https://time.com/5377386/1968-democratic-national-convention-protesters/

56 Richard Nixon 1968 Election. https://www.270towin.com/1968_Election/

57 Apollo 8 Book of Genesis. https://creation.com/apollo-8-genesis

58 Vietnam deaths. https://thevietnamwar.info/vietnam-war-casualties/

59 Tet Offensive. https://www.history.com/topics/vietnam-war/vietnam-war-history

60 Soviet spending Vietnam. https://www.history.com/topics/vietnam-war/vietnam-war-history

61 SDS. Students for a Democratic Society became ardent protesters of the War in Vietnam.

62 Service Medals. http://vets4energy.com/about-us/william-leon-schachte-jr-rear-admiral-usn-ret.html

63 CINCLANT. https://acronyms.thefreedictionary.com/CinCLANT

64 Vieques Island. https://nvdatabase.swarthmore.edu/content/puerto-ricans-force-united-states-navy-out-vieques-island-1999-2003

65 Roosevelt Roads Base. https://www.peoplesworld.org/article/navy-closes-last-base-in-puerto-rico/

66 Puerto Rican base closures. Ibid.

67 History of International Maritime Law. https://www.britannica.com/topic/maritime-law

68 IMO. https://www.govserv.org/GB/London/107878965934354/International-Maritime-Organization---IMO

69 Schachte Senate Testimony 2004.

70 Schachte Senate Testimony. https://www.foreign.senate.gov/imo/media/doc/SchachteTestimony031014.pdf

71 Gadhafi Tent Attack. https://www.politico.com/story/2019/04/15/reagan-bomb-libya-april-15-1986-1272788

72 Service Medals. http://vets4energy.com/about-us/william-leon-schachte-jr-rear-admiral-usn-ret.html

73 Soviet Mirka II Class Frigate. https://nara.getarchive.net/media/a-soviet-petya-i-class-frigate-ffl-and-an-alfa-class-nuclear-powered-fleet-b805aa

74 Ushanka hats, Soviet. blog.ushanka.us/2012/04/new-blog-concept.html

75 Black Sea Incident. https://nara.getarchive.net/media/a-soviet-petya-i-class-frigate-ffl-and-an-alfa-class-nuclear-powered-fleet-b805aa

76 Deputy DOD Ocean Policy Affairs. http://www.martindale.com/William-L-Schachte/352829-lawyer.htm

77 Soviet Treaty 1989. https://cil.nus.edu.sg/wp-content/uploads/formidable/18/1989-USA-USSR-Joint-Statement-with-Attached-Uniform-Interpretation-of-Rues-of-International-Law-Governing-Innocent-Passage.pdf

78 Ronald Reagan presidency. https://www.history.com/topics/us-presidents/ronald-reagan

79 Lt. Col. Oliver North. https://www.britannica.com/biography/Oliver-North

80 The Reagan Doctrine. https://www.history.com/this-day-in-history/the-reagan-doctrine-is-announced

81 Besame Mucho. https://culturacolectiva.com/music/besame-mucho-mexican-song-consuelo-velazquez-origin-story

82 Arthur D. Nicholson, Jr. https://www.army.mil/article/99179/major_arthur_d_nicholson_jr_becomes_last_cold_war_casualty_this_week_in_history

83 Soviet attempted coup. https://www.history.com/this-day-in-history/coup-attempt-against-gorbachev-collapses

84 General Colin Powell. https://www.biography.com/political-figure/colin-powell

85 Rivers of the Black Sea. https://en.wikipedia.org/wiki/Danube

86 Soviet Maritime Law. https://heinonline.org/HOL/LandingPage?handle=hein.journals/rsl10&div=27&id=&page=

87 Black Sea Incident of March, 1986. https://en.wikipedia.org/wiki/1986_Black_Sea_incident

88 GRU. Main Russian intelligence directorate formed after the fall of the Soviet Union in 1991.

89 Stanislav Lunev. https://en.wikipedia.org/wiki/Stanislav_Lunev

90 Russian Spying 1990. https://www.fbi.gov/investigate/counterintelligence

91 IBID.

92 KGB Operatives. https://www.washingtonpost.com/archive/politics/1985/08/04/spy-watchers-outmanned-by-communist-operatives/20a1200d-cea4-4f10-8b53-4dfc-cf407eea/

93 John Anthony Walker, Jr. https://www.washingtonpost.com/national/john-a-walker-who-led-family-spy-ring-dies/2014/08/30/dbc41a56-2f9d-11e4-bb9b-997ae96fad33_story.html

94 Aldrich Ames. https://www.washingtonpost.com

95 Dacha. https://www.themoscowtimes.com/2019/01/03/russia-disbands-the-concept-of-dacha-a64027

96 https://www.dictionary.com/browse/dacha

97 Zil Cars. https://www.motor1.com/news/64031/soviet-bloc-cars-were-weird-zil-4102/

98 USS Iowa. https://www.history.navy.mil/content/history/museums/nmusn/explore/photography/ships-us/ships-usn-i/uss-iowa-bb-61.html

99 Decommissioning. https://www.history.navy.mil/content/history/museums/nmusn/explore/photography/ships-us/ships-usn-i/uss-iowa-bb-61.html

100 IBID.

101 IBID.

102 Transport of FDR. https://www.history.navy.mil/content/history/museums/nmusn/explore/photography/ships-us/ships-usn-i/uss-iowa-bb-61.html

103 Presidential Party aboard Iowa. https://www.history.navy.mil/content/history/museums/nmusn/explore/photography/ships-us/ships-usn-i/uss-iowa-bb-61.html

104 Iowa Class. https://www.history.navy.mil/content/history/museums/nmusn/explore/photography/ships-us/ships-usn-i/uss-iowa-bb-61.html

105 USS Iowa crew. https://www.history.navy.mil/content/history/museums/nmusn/explore/photography/ships-us/ships-usn-i/uss-iowa-bb-61.html

106 Capstone. https://www.military.com/military-transition/completing-your-capstone-form.html

107 1956 Tailhook Association. https://www.pbs.org/wgbh/pages/frontline/shows/navy/tailhook/assoc.html

108 Las Vegas 1991 Tailhook Convention. https://www.britannica.com/event/Tailhook-scandal

109 Washington Post Tailhook Interview. https://www.washingtonpost.com/archive/lifestyle/tv/1995/05/21/she-stood-alone-the-tailhook-scandal/947490ae-c833-429d-b412-b4d79e514465/

110 IBID.

111 Techno Thrillers. https://www.usatoday.com/story/life/books/2013/10/02/tom-clancy-appreciation/2908305/

112 Jack Ryan. https://www.britannica.com/biography/Tom-Clancy

113 Tom Clancy Novels. https://www.britannica.com/biography/Tom-Clancy.

114 USS Iowa. https://www.navysite.de/bb/bb61.htm

115 IBID.

116 IBID.

117 Judge Advocate General. https://www.jag.navy.mil

118 Paula Coughlin testimony. https://www.orlandosentinel.com/news/os-xpm-1992-06-27-9206270953-story.html

119 Newsweek on Tailhook. http://www.newsweek.com/tailhook-scandal-time-200362

120 Election of Governor David Beasley. https://www.washingtonpost.com/wp-srv/politics/campaigns/keyraces98/stories/sc093098.htm

121 Role of Navy JAG. https://www.public.navy.mil/bupers-

122 npc/officer/communitymanagers/active/StaffCorps/Pages/JudgeAdvocateGeneralCorps(JAG).aspx

123 2004 Election. https://www.270towin.com/2004_Election/

124 IBID.

125 IBID.

126 Lisa Myers. http://premierespeakers.com/lisa_myers/bio

127 Voting numbers 2004. Ibid.

128 Antimedia Blogspot. https://antimedia.blogspot.com/2004/08/rear-admiral-schachte-breaks-his.html

129 IBID. https://antimedia.blogspot.com/2004/08/rear-admiral-schachte-breaks-his.html

130 Truth or Fiction. https://www.truthorfiction.com/kerry/

131 Terry Garlock. https://www.truthorfiction.com/kerry/

132 Patriots Post. https://patriotpost.us/pages/345-statement-of-radm-william-l-schachte-jr-usn-ret-dot

133 Patriot Post. https://patriotpost.us/pages/345-statement-of-radm-william-l-schachte-jr-usn-ret-dot

134 Congressional staffing. https://www.ncoa.org/public-policy-action/advocacy-toolkit/understanding-congress/capitol-hill-terms/

135 Hurricane Maria 2017. https://www.nationalgeographic.com/magazine/2018/03/puerto-rico-after-hurricane-maria-dispatches/

CPSIA information can be obtained
at www.ICGtesting.com
Printed in the USA
BVHW022144250620
582345BV00011B/30